SOUVENIRS

FROM ROMAN TIMES TO THE PRESENT DAY

Godfrey Evans

NMS Publishing

ACKNOWLEDGEMENTS

A wide-ranging survey such as this could not have been written and illustrated without the ground-breaking work of earlier writers and the collaboration of many other experts and owners. I am profoundly indebted to Brian Austen, Ronald Lightbown and the other authors listed in the bibliography. At the same time, I wish to express my deep gratitude to Peter Jeffs for all his help in shaping both this book and the related exhibition over the past three years. It is also a great pleasure to be able to acknowledge all the kindness and assistance I have received from: Maureen Barrie, June Baxter, Shawn P Brennan, David Caldwell, Hugh Cheape, Graeme D R Cruickshank, George Dalgleish, Margaret J Davidson, Roger Dodsworth, Nick Dolan, Julia Elton, Oliver Fairclough, John R Findlay, Leslie Florence, His Grace the Duke of Hamilton, Stanley K Hunter, Philip Jeffs, Helen Kemp, Don R Knight, Morag Lyall, Gordon McFarlan, Brenda McGoff, Alastair McKay, Susan T Moore, Frank Newby, Michael A Rix, Elizabeth Robertson, Elize Rowan, Heather Ryan, Harrie George Schloss, Ken Schultz, Joyce Smith, William H Straus and Naomi Tarrant.

Photography by Joyce Smith of NMS Photography with the exception of 17: Lennoxlove House, Haddington. 21: National Museums and Galleries of Wales, Cardiff. 61: Alan Curtis, Hartlebury, for Broadfield House Glass Museum, Kingswinford.

CONTENTS

INTRODUCTION

This book contains a sequence of chronological surveys which examine the main types of Western souvenirs of places and events from Late Roman times to the present day.

It does not cover mementoes which were given or kept as reminders of, or memorials to, relatives, friends and important individuals. Examples of these would include lockets of hair of loved ones and the carefully preserved possessions of famous soldiers and sailors. At the same time, the review avoids many 'commemoratives': pieces that commemorate an event (eg a battle or a royal coronation or wedding). Commemoratives were often made for widespread geographical distribution and are a subject in their own right. Nevertheless, it is abundantly clear that many were sold and bought as souvenirs.

The acid test for the works discussed here has been: were they, or could they have been, acquired in or near the places they relate to?

As we set out to explore the mountains of material made over the past 1,700 years, it is essential to appreciate that there are three main categories of souvenirs of places and events. First, the found natural objects, such as the stones from religious and archaeological sites and the pebbles and shells from beaches. Second, the kept normal items: travel tickets, receipts, printed programmes, beer mats, and so forth. Third, the purpose-made souvenirs.

The latter range from cheap and nasty vulgarities to expensive luxury goods, and are the souvenirs that chiefly concern us. They include many objects that are seldom recognised today as souvenirs.

It has to be said that this book is published at a very opportune time. Not only is there a growing interest in souvenirs, both in Europe and North America, but the prices on the antiques and art markets are increasing steadily and, in some cases, quite spectacularly.

A souvenir of Coney Island. Cushion cover of printed rayon, with a yellow cotton fringe, made in the United States of America in the 1950s.

PILGRIMS' PROGRESS
FROM RELICS TO SOUVENIRS

The history of Christian pilgrimage effectively begins with the Emperor Constantine the Great, who legalised Christianity in 313 and made it the dominant religion of the Roman Empire. In 324 Constantine defeated the pagan Licinius and united the western and eastern halves of the empire. Over the next few years Constantine's mother, the Empress Helena, would go on pilgrimage to Jerusalem and the emperor and empress would build the Church of the Holy Sepulchre in Jerusalem and the Church of the Nativity in Bethlehem.

Late Roman and Byzantine pilgrims were partly motivated by the belief that the sanctity of holy people, holy objects and holy places was, in some manner, transferable through physical contact. They were keen to collect the stones and earth that formed part of a holy place because they believed these items could convey and transfer a spiritual blessing. Many Christians were convinced that such pieces could actually cure and protect.

This created a very real problem for the guardians of the holy places. On the one hand, they were faced with the danger that a fervent pilgrim might damage a shrine to obtain a semi-relic – even breaking off bits of rock from Calvary or Christ's tomb in the Church of the Holy Sepulchre. On the other, there was very little that pilgrims could take from some of the sites. Over the years the guardians sought to prevent damage and to satisfy the rising demand for souvenirs and secondary relics by the controlled release of hallowed oil, earth, dust and water. Pilgrims were only allowed a small amount, which was placed in a small container, an ampulla or pilgrim-flask, and sealed up. At some stage, there may have been a rite of blessing.

The early surviving containers are generally made of clay or earthenware, with flattened oval bodies and two loops for suspension around a person's neck or body. Many are decorated with the Egyptian soldier-saint Menas, whose shrine was at Abu Mena, to the south-west of Alexandria (fig 1). They probably contained water from the many cisterns at the shrine or oil from a lamp suspended above the saint's tomb. Another group shows a man writing. Most scholars accept that he represents St John the Evangelist and link these flasks with the huge shrine of St John at Ephesus.

The pious belief here was that the saint was blowing holy dust from his tomb and that this was particularly potent – able to ensure the happy outcome of a difficult childbirth or to stop storms at sea.

As one would expect, we know most about what was happening in Jerusalem. Around 570 an anonymous pilgrim from Piacenza, in north Italy, visited the Church of the Holy Sepulchre and recorded:

> In the place where the Lord's body was laid, at the head, has been placed a bronze lamp. It burns there day and night, and we took a blessing from it, and then put it back. Earth is brought to the Tomb and put inside, and those who go in take some as a blessing.

The Piacenza pilgrim goes on to describe an impressive ceremony:

> In the courtyard of the basilica [at Golgotha] is a small room where they keep the Wood of the Cross. We venerated it with a kiss … At the moment when the Cross is brought out of the small room for veneration … a star appears in the sky, and comes over the place where they lay the Cross. It stays overhead whilst they are venerating the Cross, and they offer oil to be blessed in little flasks. When the mouth of one of the little flasks touches the Wood of the Cross, the oil instantly bubbles over, and unless it is closed very quickly it all spills out.

1 *Earthenware pilgrim-flasks showing St Menas flanked by two camels, fifth-seventh centuries. Two camels are said to have brought the martyred body of the saint to Abu Mena, where they stopped and refused to move on.*

Some of the precious oil was poured into high-quality metal ampullae. The outstanding examples are the sixteen ampullae at Monza Cathedral, which are reputed to have been presented by Queen Theodelinda of the Lombards (d 625), and the twenty fragments of similar ampullae at Bobbio Cathedral, also in north Italy. These are richly decorated in relief with the Holy Sepulchre, the Cross of Golgotha and scenes from the life of Christ and bear Greek inscriptions: 'Oil [of the] Tree of Life from the Holy Places of Christ' and 'Blessing [of the] Lord from the Holy Places of Christ'.

Ampullae were also used in Europe to collect oil burning in lamps in the shrines and catacombs in Rome and other holy places. However, the best-known European examples were made in Canterbury and contained 'Canterbury water': water tinged with the merest suspicion of St Thomas Becket's blood. After Thomas's murder in the cathedral in December 1170, the monks carefully collected the martyr's blood and soon discovered that a little of it, mixed with water, could bring about miraculous cures when drunk or applied as a lotion. Within a short time, Canterbury water was available in cast tin ampullae. Many are in the shape of scallop shells, with two small loops for suspension, but more elaborate 'sculptural' ampullae were also produced. Some of these are in the form of tiny roofed, rectangular reliquaries, while others represent the saint on the container itself and have a circular surround of openwork decoration. The healing and protective powers of the water are referred to in Latin inscriptions on thirteenth-century pieces. One group declares 'Thomas is the best doctor of the worthy sick', while another type reads 'All weakness and pain is removed, the healed man eats and drinks, and evil and death pass away'.

The growing enthusiasm for pilgrimage and the promotion of many shrines, all trying to attract the maximum number of pilgrims, led to the widespread introduction of pilgrim badges in the twelfth century and thereafter. Two natural objects had already established themselves as souvenirs and symbols of pilgrimage. The first was the palm leaf, which was the traditional symbol of pilgrimage to the Holy Land, and was on sale at stalls in Jerusalem by the twelfth century. More significantly, scallop shells had become popular with pilgrims to the shrine of St James Major at Santiago de Compostela, in north-west Spain, and were well on their way to becoming the internationally recognised symbol of a pilgrim and of pilgrimage.

2 Lead alloy ampulla found near Craigmillar Castle, Edinburgh, thirteenth century.

3 Modern replicas of pilgrim badges of St Andrew with the stone mould found in the churchyard of old St Andrew's Church, North Berwick, fourteenth century. Like Continental badges, the original Scottish badges were intended to be stitched to hats or clothing. English badges were generally pinned on.

Pilgrim badges were generally cast in tin-lead and were intended to be worn on the pilgrim's hat or clothing (fig 3). They usually represented the saint associated with the shrine and indicated a pilgrimage to that shrine. As the *Veneranda dies* sermon in the *Liber Sancti Jacobi* explains, a pilgrim badge bore witness to the pilgrim's great labour and was a sign that he had mortified his flesh and overcome his vices. To William of Tyre, writing about 1180, they were a symbol of a pilgrimage fulfilled.

The original idea was that the pilgrim bought his badge on arrival at the shrine and that the lucrative trade raised revenue for the Church authorities. Badges also served to advertise the saint and to stimulate more visitors. Sales figures are hard to come by, but great shrines such as Canterbury, Aachen and Santiago must have sold tens, if not hundreds, of thousands of badges each year. In 1466, 130,000 badges were sold, at two pfennig apiece, at the important Swiss monastery of Santa Maria, Einsiedeln, within a fortnight. The sale of 'false badges' from other sources was taken very seriously in the early period. In 1207 Pope Innocent III instructed the archbishops of Spain and Gascony to prohibit the sale of *adulterina insignia,* known as

conchae, in their territories, and to excommunicate those who continued to make and sell them. His successors reissued the prohibition in 1228, 1259, 1266 and 1272.

These merit badges obviously appealed to pilgrims. Some owners cherished their badges, taking them with them to the grave, bequeathing them or giving them to their churches or other shrines. Many people regarded them as amulets and prophylactics, placing them at entrances, at the footings of buildings, on walls, above beds, with their animals or on drinking-troughs.

Pilgrim badges may have been the first popular, mass-produced souvenirs, but they were not the only items on offer. Guidebooks and other sources reveal that pilgrims were able to buy luxury items, including cloth and gold-smiths' work, at many shrines. Nowadays, the most frequently encountered luxury souvenirs are the pieces of

4 Jet statuette of St James, Santiago de Compostela, possibly second half of the fifteenth century.

5 Pilgrim's badge with carved jet representation of St James's legendary appearance at the Battle of Clavijo, Santiago de Compostela, sixteenth or seventeenth century. Acquired by the Scottish painter Sir Joseph Noel Paton from the dealer F W Fairholt in 1848.

carved jet made for pilgrims to Santiago de Compostela. Santiago had become one of the principal shrines in Christendom by the twelfth century and was drawing an estimated half a million visitors a year at the height of its popularity in the Middle Ages. Few of the thirteenth- and fourteenth-century jet pieces have come down to us. The most common later items are the small statuettes of St James (fig 4), either alone or with one or more diminutive flanking figures, and the small amulets in the shape of a clenched hand. Much rarer are the small carvings of St James as *Santiago Matamoros* (St James the Moor-Slayer), which represent the saint's alleged intervention at the unrecorded Battle of Clavijo in 844, when he is said to have miraculously appeared on a horse, rallied the Christian troops and defeated the Muslims (fig 5). Jet carvings are difficult to date with any preci-

sion: the statuettes of St James are generally assigned to the fifteenth or sixteenth centuries, while representations of St James the Moor-Slayer are normally thought to be later. A key item, both in its own right and in helping to date other work, is the pilgrim's hat of Stephan Praun of Nuremberg. Now in the Germanisches Nationalmuseum in Nuremberg, it is decorated with small jet figures of St James, bone staves and shells acquired by Praun during his visit to Santiago in 1571.

The range of religious souvenirs expands enormously after the mid fifteenth century. This is partly due to the introduction of woodcuts and, later, other types of prints.

4

Among the earliest souvenir prints are the 'faces of Christ' or 'veronicas', which were supposed to show the face of Christ on the handkerchief of St Veronica, one of the principal relics in St Peter's in Rome. These were being sold by Germans, the originators of the woodcut, from booths on both sides of the main door of St Peter's in the mid 1470s. From the early sixteenth century, pilgrims were able to buy copperplate engravings of religious images, views of shrines and centres, and illustrated lists of relics and treasures owned by cathedrals and churches. In the nineteenth century there was a major shift to small, easily portable images, printed from copper or steel plates.

The later religious souvenirs are often much more interesting than the earlier items. Take, for instance, the small tin-glazed earthenware bowls (fig 6), which were made for pilgrims to the famous shrine of Loreto, near Ancona in Italy. They had come to see the house of the Virgin Mary at Nazareth (allegedly transported to Loreto by angels after 1295), a venerated statue of the Virgin, and a bowl – the *Santa Scodella* – said to have been used by Mary. The colourful souvenirs allude to the bowl and are painted, on the sides, with the abbreviated inscription 'CON POLVERE DI SANTA CASA' or 'CON POLVERE ET AQUA DI SANTA CASA' (with dust and water from the Holy House). In other words, they have some dust, and possibly some water, from the Holy House mixed in the actual ceramic body. In 1868

6 Maiolica or tin-glazed earthenware bowls painted with the Virgin and Child for pilgrims to Loreto, eighteenth or nineteenth century. Both examples were purchased at Dowell's sale-room in Edinburgh in 1897.

On the plate: ONSE LIVE VROUW TOT KEVELAAR

7 *Cream-coloured earthen-ware plate painted in enamels with 'Our Lady of Kevelaer'. The plate was probably made in Leeds and decorated in the Netherlands, c1780.*

Joseph Marryat described how

> When the chapel is swept, the dust shaken from the dress of the Virgin, or scraped from the walls, is carefully collected, and mixed with the paste, out of which are made small cups, about four inches in diameter and one-and-a-half inch high.

Most of these bowls were made either in Loreto or at a nearby centre in the Marches.

Some of the souvenirs on sale at Kevelaer, in the Lower Rhineland, also merit special attention. The cult of the Virgin of Kevelaer is centred on a miracle-working engraving of the Virgin of Luxembourg, dated 1640, which was set up in a small shrine, then in a chapel, at Kevelaer in the 1640s. According to some accounts, the print was attracting 100,000 visitors a year during the first half of the eighteenth century. During this

6

period, local potters at Sonsbeck, Sevelen and Tönisberg were producing 'folk art' plates and bowls of coloured, glazed earthenware, decorated with the Virgin of Kevelaer, and also small statuettes and shrines.

In the late eighteenth century people with more sophisticated taste were able to buy cream-coloured earthenware plates and tea services, painted in polychrome enamels with the Virgin of Kevelaer (fig 7). The bases of some of these items are impressed either 'TURNER' for the Staffordshire potter John Turner (1738-86) of Lane End, or his sons, or with one of the Leeds Pottery marks. Other pieces can be attributed to Staffordshire or Leeds on the basis of their patterns, the colour of the earthenware or the appearance of the glaze. The enamel colours and style of decoration indicate that these ceramics were exported 'plain' to the Netherlands and decorated there. It seems that Dutch merchants played a seminal role in producing these souvenirs and transporting them to Kevelaer. This is not as surprising as one might think: Kevelaer lies on the trade route between Amsterdam and Cologne and was visited by many Dutch pilgrims.

Among the other Kevelaer souvenirs are items for smoking and snuff-taking. The most common are the oval tobacco-boxes (fig 8), engraved with the Virgin of Kevelaer on the lid and St Anthony of Padua on the base. They are stylistically 'Dutch' and are engraved in Dutch with the identities of the two figures and the inscription (below the Virgin): 'Come pilgrims, honour this Virgin with diligence; then she will hear your prayer before you return. She is the advocate for us all, therefore visit her at Kevelaer.' Once again, it looks as though Dutch merchants were involved with this type of souvenir.

Nevertheless, the most remarkable later souvenirs must be the ones made in the Holy Land. Sadly, very little is known about the purpose-made souvenirs available to fifteenth- and sixteenth-century pilgrims, including those who came on the 'package tours' organised by the Venetians. However, from at least the 1660s, there are dozens of large wooden models of the Church of the Holy Sepulchre, which are decorated with inlaid mother-of-pearl and bone in the tradition of Islamic, and particularly Syrian, intarsia work. Most have the arms of Jerusalem on the courtyard and the Sacred Monogram 'IHS' on the bell tower.

8 *Brass tobacco-box engraved with 'Our Lady of Kevelaer', eighteenth century.*

7

9 *Wooden model of the Cave or Grotto of the Nativity under the Church of the Nativity, Bethlehem, inlaid with mother-of-pearl and bone. Made in Bethlehem or Jerusalem in the eighteenth or nineteenth century and bought at Chapman's auction-house in Edinburgh by the Royal Museum in 1880. The five Maltese crosses on the lid are the arms of Jerusalem.*

10 *Wooden cross and rosary with mother-of-pearl decoration, Jerusalem or Bethlehem, eighteenth century, with German or Bohemian silver mounts. Given to Sir Joseph Noel Paton in Karlsbad in 1868.*

There are also small models of the Cave of the Nativity in Bethlehem (fig 9), hundreds of eighteenth- and nineteenth-century altar and table crosses, and thousands of crucifixes and rosaries with mother-of-pearl decoration (fig 10). Some of these items are decorated with the arms of the Franciscan Order, as well as the Sacred Monogram and arms of Jerusalem.

The majority of these items would have been made by Arab-Christian craftsmen and their families, either working directly for the Franciscans – the Latin or western custodians of the Christian places in the Holy Land since the fourteenth century – or with much looser links with the order. Other nineteenth-century souvenirs include pearloyster shells carved with scenes from the life of Christ and other religious subject-matter (fig 11) and crosses, cups and bowls of bitumen.

11 *Pearl-oyster shell carved with St Anne educating the Virgin Mary. This was one of two shells purchased 'at the door of the Holy Sepulchre', which were given to the Royal Museum in 1860. The museum register records that they were 'the work of the monks in the neighbourhood of Jerusalem'.*

All these types of souvenirs could have been purchased in the vicinity of the Church of the Holy Sepulchre and elsewhere in Jerusalem, but there is also abundant evidence that the Franciscans and others were engaged in a well-developed and profitable export trade. Constantin Volney, who visited the Holy Land in 1784, states that 'about three hundred boxes' of rosaries, reliquaries, shrines, crosses, crucifixes, Agnus Deis, scapulars, etc, were exported from Jerusalem each year to Turkey, Italy, Portugal, Spain and its colonies. Writing of his visit in 1806, the German Ulrich Jasper Seetzen refers specifically to a warehouse in the convent of St Saviour, the Franciscans' main base in Jerusalem. He records that it contained 'religious articles such as rosaries, crucifixes, Madonna's Milk, models of the Holy Sepulchre, etc', which were 'sent through agents to Italy, Spain and Portugal'. According to the English engraver W H Bartlett, items worth several thousands of pounds were being shipped each year to France, Italy, Spain and Austria in the mid nineteenth century.

It is therefore important to separate 'souvenirs' of the Holy Land into items that were definitely acquired by pilgrims, and undocumented pieces, which may be part of the international export trade and a precursor to today's mail-order business.

SPA SOUVENIRS

Some of the earliest purpose-made secular souvenirs were made for wealthy visitors to spas, who frequently had little to do between bouts of drinking the waters and must have been delighted to shop for luxury goods and mementoes.

At Spa itself, in the wooded hilly Ardennes in what is now Belgium, the souvenir industry seems to have developed from the production of walking staffs or staves. These long sticks became popular with visitors, and the town authorities presented *bastons* or *bordons* to various dignitaries between at least 1600 and 1675. Brushes and bellows, which can be viewed as transitional items, are recorded as gifts in the 1620s and 1630s. By the late seventeenth century, caskets or large boxes had become the salient pieces (fig 12).

Many late seventeenth-century products were decorated with mother-of-pearl. In 1672, for example, there is an account, in the local archive: *'Pour une belle eschouvette travaillée de nacre de perles. 4 florins 10 patars'*. In 1703 another account refers to *'deux casettes travaillées d'estain et de perles que j'ai achetées à l'Echevin Xhrouet pour 15 escus'*. Edmond Nessel provides some useful information about late seventeenth- to early eighteenth-century wares in his *Traîté des Eaux de Spa*, published in 1699. He notes:

> They work also very nicely with all sorts of colours as well as with mother-of-pearl, ivory, tortoiseshell, tin of Cornwall, copper and silver. They are also imitating there, and they produce just as cleverly as in any other place, works of marquetry representing all sorts of figures, of men and animals, insects, flowers, foliages and all that one can desire.

These descriptions can be linked to caskets, mirrors and other items, decorated with inlaid engraved and painted mother-of-pearl and brass wire, now in the Musée de la Ville d'Eaux at Spa. Many more pieces can be attributed to Spa by comparison with this core group. Some must have been made by the Xhrouet family, who seem to have been the leading makers in these materials in the late seventeenth century and were apparently still employing and decorating mother-of-pearl in 1734. Exact dating is difficult. A bellows decorated with mother-of-pearl and brass wire, dated 1658, suggests that this type of decoration was well developed by the late

1650s, while entries in the archives imply that it was still being used in the early eighteenth century.

During the 1680s and 1690s there is also clear evidence that some craftsmen were imitating the Oriental lacquer being imported into Europe by the East India Companies. Roussel supplied *'deux casettes de la verny de la Chine'* in 1689, and Nessel observes: 'It is a pleasure to see thousands of niceties made in lacquer, done à la façon des Indes.' He mentions both flat and raised work, the use of many colours, gilt embellishment and highly polished finishes. Oriental-style lacquer continued to be produced in the eighteenth century. Baron Pöllnitz, who visited Spa in 1729, admired the way the lacquermasters 'mimic Japan so exactly that it is difficult to tell the difference'. The emphasis on amusement and the bizarre during the rococo period led to a revival of Oriental-style lacquer at Spa in the mid eighteenth century.

By the 1720s there was a considerable variety of painted and varnished items. Gérard Dagly is credited with discovering the special Spa varnish in the late seventeenth century, and by the late 1720s a high percentage of the population of Spa was manufacturing and selling 'knick-knacks' (to use Baron Pöllnitz's term). Pöllnitz visited a dozen shops in the company of ladies in 1729 and declared that the Xhrouet excelled at fables and history,

12 *Wooden casket inlaid with engraved and painted mother-of-pearl and brass wire, attributed to Spa, about 1680.*

the Leloup at landscapes and perspective, while Dagly at the White Pigeon (presumably a relation of Gérard Dagly) made the best varnish and had 'a special taste for fruits and flowers, whether flat or embossed'. The most highly prized acquisition, at least for the ladies, was a complete toilet set, with boxes of various sizes. Pöllnitz briefly describes some examples, including one 'raised with gold foliage and with arms and cypher on every box' and another 'in blue like lapis lazuli with landskips in camayeu'. Among the wide range of other items were cases for tweezers, scissors or watches, boxes for pins, gambling counters or tobacco, dessert trays, work-baskets, necklaces and canes.

The main development in the second half of the eighteenth century was the production of small rectangular boxes and other items decorated with one or more views of the spas or other sights in and around Spa. These views are normally identified and were generally executed in Indian ink or monochrome washes, either directly on to the wood or on to paper or parchment which was attached to the piece. Such work may have originated with Remacle Leloup (1711-49), who produced illustrations for *Les Délices du Pays de Liège* and may be the Leloup praised by Pöllnitz in 1729 for 'landskips and perspective'. Some views are close, in style and form, to published illustrations and drawings by his son, Antoine Leloup (1730-?1802). The surrounds and borders on the boxes are usually comparatively pale and plain, but can be quite elaborate, with coloured marbling or bands of small repeating motifs. Nineteenth-century decorators employed a rich palette of colours and endeavoured to create miniature oil paintings. In the late eighteenth century, Spa craftsmen also made and decorated small pieces of furniture, such as tables, corner cupboards for hanging on walls and candlestands.

Wooden souvenirs were also available at the 'courtiers' spa' of Tunbridge Wells in Kent, which was easily reached from London. The spring was probably 'discovered' by Dudley, third Lord North, in 1606 and was visited by Queen Henrietta Maria in 1629. After the restoration of the monarchy, Tunbridge was patronised by King Charles II, Queen Catherine of Braganza and other members of the royal family. Shops were opened in the 1660s and 1670s, but the main development took place in the 1680s and 1690s. Following a fire in 1687, the Upper Walk was rebuilt in the form of a continuous colonnade with shops behind it. It was here, in 1697, that the traveller Celia Fiennes found 'shopps full of all sorts of toys, silver, china, milliners, and all sorts of curious wooden ware, which this place is noted for'. She goes on to describe the treen as 'a delicate neate and thin ware of wood both white and Lignum vitae wood'.

Until recently, it was thought that some or all of these pieces were made by George Wise of Tonbridge, a turner and the founder of a dynasty of Tunbridge ware makers. However, it is now known that he was not born until 1703 and did not lease premises until 1746. The working theory is that many of the early wares were made by London craftsmen and were brought to Tunbridge for sale. This view is based on three considerations. In the first place, lignum vitae is a hardwood imported from the West Indies and tropical America and the sort of wood one would expect London, rather than Tunbridge, makers to be using in the 1680s-1690s. Second, the silver and some of the other items mentioned by Celia Fiennes and her contemporaries probably came from London. Third, Londoners were heavily involved with the expansion and commercialisation of Tunbridge. The main developers included Thomas Ashenhurst of Lambeth and Sir Thomas Janson of St Martin-in-the-Fields, and many lesser figures traded with the spa and rented shops.

The number of turners recorded in the Tunbridge area in the first half of the eighteenth century suggests that much of the early, locally-made Tunbridge ware was turned on the lathe, and consisted of cups, goblets, bowls, plates, circular boxes, ladles and 'toys'. Small cabinet work was also produced and became increasingly important. In his *History of Tunbridge Wells*, published in 1766, Thomas Benge Burr states:

> The trade of Tunbridge-Wells is similar to that of the Spa in Germany [ie Spa in Belgium], and chiefly consists in a variety of toys in wood, such as tea-chests, dressing-boxes, snuff-boxes, punch-ladles, and numerous other little articles of the same kind. Of these great quantities are sold to the company in the summer, and especially at their leaving the place, when it is customary for them to take Tunbridge fairings to their friends at home.
>
> This ware takes its name from the place, on account of its employing a great number of hands, and being made there in a much neater manner than any where else in England. The wood principally used for this purpose is holly, which grows in great abundance in the surrounding country, and furnishes a prodigious variety of the prettiest ornamental inlays that can be imagined, some of which are so excellent in their kind, that it is hard to believe they are not assisted by the pencil. But, besides holly, they use no small quantity of cherry-tree, plum-tree, yew, and sycamore: the yew especially is of late become very fashionable, and the goods vineered with it are certainly excessively pretty.

Veneering led to the production of tea caddies and other items decorated with good-quality marquetry in the late eighteenth century and then to boxes and other articles adorned with cube and other types of parquetry in the early nineteenth century. At the same time, manufacturers were making whitewood boxes and other pieces decorated with paint, prints or

13 *Marquetry mosaic picture of the Pantiles, Tunbridge Wells, attributed to the manufactory of Henry Hollamby (closed c1891) or the factory of Boyce, Brown & Kemp, Tunbridge Wells, late nineteenth or early twentieth century. Bought at Tunbridge 'in the summer of 1903 by Joseph Taylor of Kansas, U.S.A., and given to his Brother'.*

penwork (or a combination of these), which were cheaper and easier to produce. During the 1830s and 1840s, Tunbridge ware underwent a fundamental change and became synonymous with work decorated with mosaic pictures or patterns cut from blocks assembled from sticks of different colours. The three most common pictures on Victorian Tunbridge ware represent the Pantiles, Tunbridge Wells (fig 13); Battle Abbey Gatehouse; and Eridge Castle. Victorian Tunbridge wares often have borders based on Berlin woolwork patterns.

By the 1840s, however, the spa had declined in popularity and manufacturers were relying more and more on a different clientele and on sales to stockists in other towns and seaside resorts.

A basic point to note about many of the items produced at Spa and Tunbridge is that they almost literally grew from the rich woodlands surrounding them. Many other spa souvenirs are also closely related to a local resource, craft or industry. In the eighteenth century visitors to the famous spa at Karlsbad (now Karlovy Vary in the Czech Republic) were able to buy folding knives, forks and spoons, and other small objects, made of iron. These were damascened with gold and silver, on russeted or fire-blued grounds, and were spin-offs from the local manufacture of guns for the Western and Turkish markets (fig 14). At Cheltenham, Isaac Cook,

Thomas Rich and other retailers were able to obtain tumblers, mugs, cups, spill vases, bough or bulb pots and other items decorated with views of Cheltenham and its spas from the Chamberlain porcelain factory at Worcester, about twenty miles away (fig 15).

This, though, merely sets the stage for the Bohemian glass industry, which did most to meet the needs and demands of the spas and their visitors. Makers, engravers and merchants in Bohemia and Silesia (in the south of Poland) supplied their local spas with functional glassware and with glasses wheel-engraved with views of the spa buildings. One of the most impressive eighteenth-century examples is a wineglass of about 1740 which shows the bathhouse at Warmbrunn, the most popular spa in Silesia. Attributed to Silesia on grounds of style, it is now in Passau Glass Museum, in the south of Germany.

Glass-engravers were active in most Bohemian spa towns, with leading practitioners working in the principal spas. The great Dominik Biemann (1800-57) spent his summers at Franzensbad (now Františkovy Lázně) engraving portraits of visitors on beakers and medallions, and selling beakers decorated with mythological, religious and equestrian subjects. As one would expect, Karlsbad was particularly well served. Biemann's chief contemporaries there were A H Mattoni (1779-1864), whose skill was praised by Goethe, and his pupil A H Pfeiffer (1801-66), who employed fifteen engravers, five glass-blowers and five painters. Ludovík Moser

14 *Flintlock revolving holster pistol attributed to Karlsbad, c1730-40, with Karlsbad-type spoons and fork, c1730-50.*

15 *Three-footed French-style cabinet cup painted in enamels with Sherbourne Spa, Cheltenham, by H & R Chamberlain & Co, Worcester, c1820.*

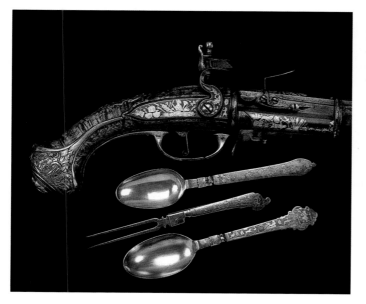

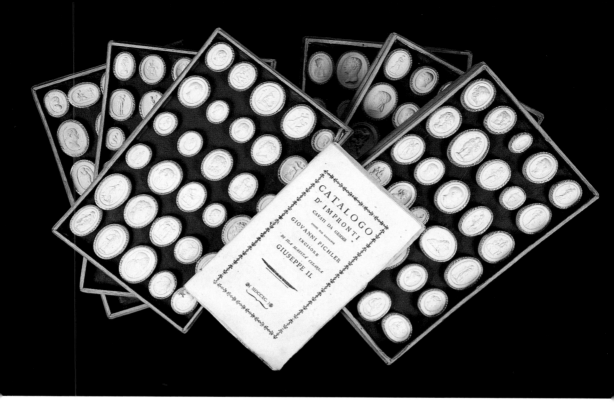

Starke's Continental guide for English travellers recommends a number of places for casts, particularly Pavoletti in the Piazza di Spagna, the famous tourist area where the British traditionally stayed.

Cameo shells (shells engraved with decoration in relief) became popular in the early nineteenth century, partly because they were easier to engrave than gem-stones and complemented neoclassical Empire-style costume very effectively. The main shell engraver in the first half of the century was Giovanni (Johann) Dies (1776-1849). An anonymous young British traveller purchased a shell cameo from him in 1821, and lamented the high price. Charlotte Eaton observed, a few years earlier, that 'the subjects are chiefly taken from ancient gems, and sometimes from sculpture and painting.'

In 1862 Murray's *Handbook of Rome* recommends Saulini of Via Babuino, 'now perhaps the first in Rome'. This was the shop of Tommaso Saulini (1793-1864) and his son Luigi. Tommaso had studied in Thorvaldsen's studio and exhibited at the 1851 Great Exhibition. In 1862 he was in the middle of a series of hardstone and shell cameo portraits for Queen Victoria and the recipient of a medal for the twenty examples of his work exhibited at the International Exhibition in London. The *Handbook* reflects the vogue for portrait cameos in the mid nineteenth

19 *Two wooden boxes with two hundred and sixteen casts of gems engraved by Giovanni Pichler mounted in ten stacking trays. The catalogue, published in 1790, contains a printed list of two hundred casts followed by a handwritten list of the sixteen additional* impronti *or impressions.*

century: Saulini is 'celebrated for his portraits', while Neri, of Piazza di Spagna, is 'also a good artist for likenesses'.

The casts after gems and the shell cameos were popular, but they are overshadowed by the success of micromosaics (fig 20). Micromosaics were developed by mosaicists employed by the Vatican Mosaic Workshop, who began to fear for their jobs as orders for large-scale mosaics began to dry up in the 1750s. The mosaicists needed to 'diversify' and began to make small-scale mosaics, which could be commissioned or bought by the Pope, cardinals, collectors and visitors. It has been said that the grand tour saved the Vatican mosaicists from unemployment.

A micromosaic is built up of hundreds or thousands of minute tesserae – cubes or chips – of coloured glass, with as many as 1,400 tesserae per square inch in some pieces. The credit for inventing or at least advancing and commercialising this type of work is generally given to Giacomo Raffaelli (1753-1836), who was one of a long line of family members employed by the Vatican Mosaic Workshop. According to Moroni, writing in 1847, Raffaelli exhibited examples of *smalti filati* – mosaics made with cut threads of coloured glass – in his private studio in Piazza di Spagna in 1775. Micromosaic workshops began to be established in and around the Piazza. In 1817 Charlotte Eaton found

20 *Roman micromosaics. Unmounted micromosaics of the 'Temple of Minerva Medica' (the early fourth-century AD pavilion in the Licinian Gardens in Rome) and the 'Doves of Pliny' mosaic. Micromosaic of a dog mounted on a box of granodiorite. The small cube-shaped tesserae in straight rows indicate that these three micromosaics were made in the late eighteenth or early nine-teenth century. Micromosaic of the Forum Romanum mounted on a box of porphyry with silver-gilt mounts by Camillo Picconi (master 1792-d1826), 1815-26. Picconi's mark, C 62 P in a lozenge, is found on many mounts for micromosaics. Bracelet decorated with micromosaics of classical buildings, flowers and figures, c1830-40.*

> hundreds of artists, or rather artisans, who carry on the manufactory of mosaics on a small scale. Snuff-boxes, rings, necklaces, brooches, ear-rings, &c. are made in immense quantity; and since the English flocked in such numbers to Rome, all the streets leading to the Piazza di Spagna, are lined with the shops of these *Musaicisti*.

A later guidebook reveals that there were at least twenty mosaic work-shops in the vicinity of the Piazza around 1873-4, all frequented by tourists.

Many late eighteenth- and early nineteenth-century micromosaics show views of classical buildings, some based on the hundred small engravings of the antiquities of Rome by Domenico Pronti, published in the late eighteenth century. Another favourite subject was the Roman mosaic called *The Doves of Pliny*, which represents four doves drinking from a bowl. Discovered at Tivoli in 1737, this was subsequently installed in the Capitoline Museum in Rome. Micromosaics of animals are also common. Many reproduce compositions after the Bohemian animal painter Wenceslaus Peter, who was active in Rome from 1774 until his death in 1829. St Peter's became increasingly popular during the nine-teenth century. It was also possible to buy painting-like plaques and tables decorated with separate scenes, a panorama, or flowers. These took anything from a few weeks to five years to complete and may have had to be ordered.

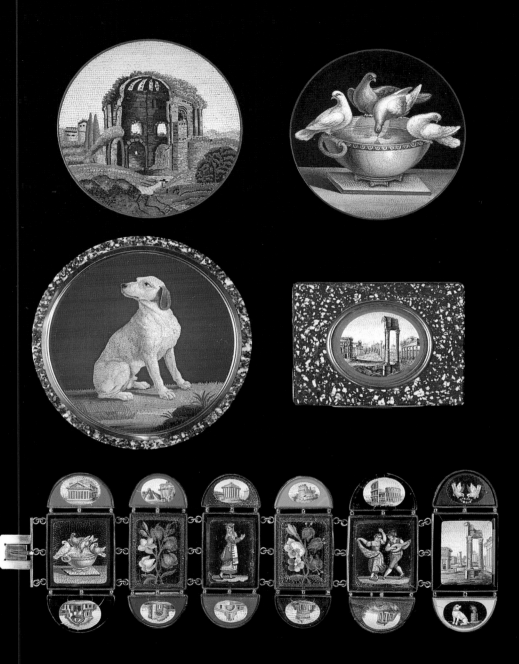

Among the other popular Roman souvenirs were artificial pearls known as 'Roman pearls' (although they were also a speciality of Naples). They were alabaster beads coated with wax which were dipped into an essence of fish scales – or something equally unpleasant. After visiting a 'manufactory of Roman pearls' in 1821, the anonymous British writer reports that the beads were finally 'dipped into a sort of viscous liquid, being the prepared entrails of a fish found only in these parts, and which gives the exact, natural lustre and hue of the real pearl'. The alleged uniqueness of the fish makes one suspect that he was repeating the sales pitch rather than accurate information. In 1829 Marianna Starke recommends the pearls sold by Pozzi, in Via Pasquino, with the warning that 'those made and sold in Via Padella and other places, are of a very inferior quality, and liable to turn yellow'.

Visitors were also keen to buy the classical archaeological-revival jewellery, which had become fashionable following the excavation of large quantities of classical jewellery, buried in tombs, in the second quarter of the nineteenth century. The pioneer in this field was Fortunato Pio Castellani (1794-1865), the founder of the famous firm of Castellani. Castellani and his sons, Alessandro and Augusto, benefited greatly from the friendship of the archaeologist and antiquarian Michelangelo Caetani, Duke of Sermoneta, who designed many pieces. They were also extremely fortunate to be able to study – as restorers and cataloguers – the major collection of antique jewellery assembled by another friend, the Marchese Giampietro Campana (which was sold in 1859-60 and is now mostly in the Louvre). Castellani's close study of classical jewellery resulted in the revival of long-forgotten techniques such as granulation, which were employed on their archaeological-revival jewellery.

A long satirical piece published in *Punch* in 1859 – purporting to be the letter of a young lady about the recent purchases in Rome of one Imogen Random – demonstrates the popularity of Castellani's 'Etruscan' jewellery and items decorated with early Christian devices in the late 1850s. In 1862 Murray's *Handbook* advises readers that Castellani

> is of European celebrity for his reproductions from the Greek, Etruscan, and ancient models generally, for the several beautiful designs of the Duke of Sermoneta… and for the imitation of early Christian and Byzantine ornaments. It is impossible to surpass in taste and beauty some of his works, which, although perhaps a little more expensive, are unrivalled amongst the Roman jewellers.

Murray's *Handbook* also recommends Castellani's rival Ernesto Pierret, 'now one of the first artists in Rome for imitations of Etruscan Jewellery, in some respect equal to Castellani, and perhaps more moderate in his prices'. An even wider range of historical-revival jewellery was made by

Castellani under the direction of Augusto Castellani (1839-1914), who had a scholarly interest in antiquities and was an honorary director of the Capitoline Museum.

The artists and makers of Florence, Venice and Naples also made great efforts to provide tourists with souvenirs, although they never matched the range on offer in Rome.

They met the tourists' paramount requirement for views of the cities with first-rate work in the eighteenth century. In Venice the presence of many travellers and tourists had encouraged and sustained the development of a school of *vedute* painters. This had, in effect, been founded by Luca Carlevarijs (1663-1730) and led on to the superlative paintings of Canaletto, his nephew and assistant Bellotto, and Francesco Guardi. As well as the paintings by these and lesser artists, there was also a plethora of prints, including the 104 etchings of buildings and views by Carlevarijs, published in 1703, and engravings and etchings after Canaletto by Marieschi, Visentini and Brustolini.

At Naples the first Earl of Seaforth was able to commission Pietro Fabris (active 1754-1804) to paint gouache views of his rooms and the entrance to the grotto at Posilippo, while the study of Vesuvius by the British ambassador, Sir William Hamilton, fuelled the demand for views of the volcano. During the late eighteenth and nineteenth centuries dozens of artists produced individual views of Vesuvius and sets of paintings showing the different stages of volcanic eruptions. Camillo da Vito painted some of the finest gouaches of Vesuvius and the classical sites in the south of Italy in the early nineteenth century, and examples are associated with a number of British families.

Unfortunately, the quality of souvenir *vedute* declined in the nineteenth century. The move from oil to gouache was followed by mounting pressure to keep the price down. This could be achieved by employing a quick, deft approach, but ran the risk of turning the artist into a repetitive (if well paid) hack. Francesco Guardi's son Giacomo (1764-1835) was reduced to churning out squiggly sketches of the Grand Canal, measuring six by nine-and-a half inches, which are only a few steps away from colour postcards and snapshot photographs.

During the second half of the century photographs and picture postcards superseded paintings and prints. The painters and print-makers did not, of course, suddenly disappear. Nor were large commercial photographic processing and printing operations set up overnight. The old and new competed. Murray's *Handbook for Travellers in Southern Italy*, of 1874, mirrors the reality of the situation and commends both the 'capital'

21 *Plate of* lattimo *or opaque-white glass painted in iron-red enamel with a view of the Grand Canal, after an engraving by Antonio Visentini of a painting by Canaletto. Probably made at the Miotti glasshouse on Murano in 1741 and owned by the ninth Earl of Lincoln.*

photographs at Sommer & Behles and the gouache views at Gatti & Dura and Pira, in Naples.

Many of the souvenirs on offer in Venice, Florence and Naples were made by the major 'speciality' crafts of the cities. In Venice the speciality was, and remains, glass. Since at least the fifteenth century, visitors had been buying glass made on the island of Murano, in the Venetian lagoon. The outstanding eighteenth-century glass souvenirs are the three sets of white glass plates painted in red enamel with views of Venice, copied from

Carlevarijs' etchings of 1703 and Visentini's engravings after Canaletto (fig 21). They appear to have been commissioned, as sets of twenty-four, by Horace Walpole, John Chute (the owner of The Vyne, near Basingstoke in Hampshire) and the ninth Earl of Lincoln (who became the second Duke of Newcastle) during their stay in Venice in 1741. All three sets were probably made at the Miotti glasshouse, which is known to have been specialising in white glass objects with decoration in enamel colours in this period. Part of John Chute's set survives at The Vyne (which is now owned by the National Trust), but the other sets are widely dispersed in public collections. Contemporary letters also record visitors buying glass knife and fork handles imitating lapis lazuli in the mid eighteenth century.

The quality of Venetian glass deteriorated after this date. Dr Johnson's friend, Mrs Hester Lynch Piozzi, was dismissive in 1785:

> here may be seen glasses of all colours, all sorts, and all prices, I believe: but whoever has looked upon the London work in this way, will not be easily dazzled by the lustre of Venetian crystal; and whoever has seen the Paris mirrors, will not be astonished at any breadth into which glass can be spread.

Napoleon's Italian campaign in the 1790s, and the disruption of trade and travel in the early nineteenth century, dealt a mortal blow to many of the forty-six glasshouses on Murano.

It is therefore understandable that the attention of visitors in the first half of the nineteenth century was focused on fine gold chains rather than on glass. Henry Matthews visited Venice in the late 1810s and noted:

> One of the principal manufactures is that of gold chain, which is brought to the greatest perfection. The price of the chain is in proportion to its diminutiveness. I gave twenty francs for a small specimen, not more than an inch and a half long, of the *ne plus ultra* of this manufacture: it is worked with the aid of microscopic glasses, and seems to be the absolute minimum of all that is little.

In 1840 the Rev T H White inspected the 'Manufactory of fine Gold Chains' and was even more astounded:

> I beheld the large fingers of a man take a snip of this fine film of gossamer, not half so long as my little finger-nail, and mould it into a fairy link, which almost demands microscopic vision to distinguish, but which he executed by the naked eye.

The glass industry began to revive in the second quarter of the nineteenth century, with glass-makers such as Domenico Bussolin, Lorenzo Radi and Francesco Torcellan re-establishing forgotten techniques and developing new glass colours. Antonio Salviati (1816-90) played a cardinal role in the revival in the late 1850s, when he founded a company to manufacture mosaics and placed the direction of the workshop under Lorenzo Radi. The venture proved very successful and was employing over 200 workers by 1862. Almost from the start, Radi was making vessel glass, which became highly regarded throughout Europe in the 1860s and 1870s (fig 22). Once again, 'Venice' was synonymous with 'glass'.

Florence had more specialities than Venice in the nineteenth century. The anonymous British traveller of 1821 tells us that

> Florence is famed for its cheapness of sculpture, as well as for the many professors of it; and, in truth, it is no little amusement to go from Studio to Studio, and admire the innumerable, and some admirable copies in alabaster and marble, from all celebrated originals, modern, or antique; as well as vases, tripods, with every other species of elegant, and fanciful, embellishment.

Four years earlier, Henry Matthews had gone round Lorenzo Bartolini's studio and remarked: 'It is now the fashion among the English to sit to him; and you find all your acquaintance drawn up in fearful array, in hard marble;- some at full length!'

Our anonymous friend may also have been tempted to sit to Bartolini, but he ended up purchasing 'two large, and beautiful, Alabaster Vases' from his studio. In the mid nineteenth century tourists could commission easily transportable, small-scale busts from the English sculptor Charles Francis Fuller (1830-75), or buy copies of antique, neoclassical and contemporary sculpture, including genre statues (such as a street urchin smoking), from the Galleria Bazzanti, run by Pietro Bazzanti (1842- 81).

An even more significant speciality, as far as souvenirs are concerned, was *pietre dure*. This literally means 'hard stones' and refers to semi-precious stones which have been cut and pieced together, like a jigsaw puzzle, to create a picture or design.

Pietre dure is an expensive art form and was used to demonstrate high status and power. The Florentine industry had developed with massive financial support from the Medici family, which ruled Florence until 1737. In 1588 Ferdinando I de' Medici, Grand Duke of Tuscany, had established a court workshop for making *pietre dure* table-tops and all the mosaics needed for the planned dynastic mausoleum at San Lorenzo. The foundation stone was finally laid in 1604 and the sheathing of the walls and floors with *pietre dure* took over two centuries.

Eighteenth-century grand tourists could acquire caskets and other items from the private workshops that had been set up over the years. A privileged minority was even able to buy or commission pieces from the court workshop, with the permission of the Medici or the governors of the House of Lorraine (which succeeded the Medici).

In 1827 John Sinclair discovered that 'Several clever artists are also employed in the pietre dura and mosaic manufactories, which are very

22 *Venetian glass bought from Salviati in 1874 and 1879.*

flourishing'. The tourist market became increasingly important as the court spent less and less on art and the Grand Duchy came to an end in 1859, as part of the unification of Italy.

In 1875 Murray's *Handbook for Travellers in Central Italy* advises readers that

> This manufacture is peculiar to Florence, and consists in general of groups of flowers and fruit, made of hard materials, generally coloured agate, quartz, lapis lazuli, cornelian, chalcedony, &c.: the operation being a most tedious one, the price is very considerable.

Among the list of the best makers are Bazzanti (fig 23), who we have met already, and 'Bosi'. This was Enrico Bosi, who was patronised by Vittorio Emanuele II and was made an equerry to the king.

Murray's *Handbook* also reminds us that, in 1875, Florence's principal industries were 'straw-platting and straw-hat making, of which manufacture it is one of the chief centres, and silk-weaving'. The straw hats and bonnets

23 Pietre dure *mosaic picture of two lovers, entitled 'The Declaration', by Pierre Bazzanti et fils, Florence, purchased in 1878 for £20.*

of Nannucci, Porta Rossa, and Porcinai, Via Tornabuoni, are highlighted, with the note that 'Most of the dealers in these celebrated articles are in the Via Porta Rossa'.

An even wider selection of souvenirs was on offer in Naples. The eighteenth-century Neapolitan speciality was tortoiseshell. Robert Adam bought three 'very handsome snuff-boxes of yellow and black tortoise-shell studded with gold' as mementoes in 1755, and in 1771 Lady Anne Miller confided:

> this city is famous for a manufacture in tortoise-shell, which they inlay curiously with gold, and are very ingenious at representing any object you choose. I have had a comb made for my *chignon* incrusted with gold, to imitate an Etruscan border, copied from an antique vase, which is so well done, that we have bespoke several other articles.

In the nineteenth century the main Neapolitan specialities were carved coral, shell cameos and 'lava' jewellery and other items, which were generally made out of coloured limestones (fig 24). By the early 1880s there were forty factories processing coral at Torre del Greco (outside Naples) employing 3,200 people. Murray's 1874 *Handbook* recommends Squadrilli, 'one of the largest and best assorted dealers in coral at Naples, and with fixed prices; he is a large exporter to the United States; he also sells lava and tortoise-shell works'.

As one would expect, copies of classical antiquities were also available in Naples. The city has a tradition of producing copies of classical jewellery. Writing in 1883, J P Rossignol traced the manufacture of forgeries back to at least 1761 and pointed a finger at the goldsmith Carlo Gropalesi. Alessandro Castellani, the eldest son of Fortunato Pio Castellani and a major dealer in antiquities, regarded a jeweller called Sarno as one of the first Neapolitan craftsmen to specialise in classicising jewellery.

In 1828 Richard, Duke of Buckingham and Chandos, visited the 'manufactory of terracotta' and commented:

> The models are all from the antique, lamps, paterae, stoves, &c. and copied from the originals in the Museo Borbonico. They are very beautiful and classical. They are fabricated from the same clay with which the ancient lamps and Etruscan wares were constructed, but cannot rival the antique. The articles which they make are one-third heavier than the ancient models.

24 *'Lava' statuette, Naples, c1862. This is 92mm high and of exceptional quality. More typical products included bracelets with small cameo heads of Italian poets or Roman Emperors, and other articles of jewellery.*

A few days later he succumbed and bought 'a few specimens for presents'.

A decade later, an English visitor complained about the guides waiting for travellers at the gates of Pozzuoli:

> These fellows plague you with medallions, and coins, and effigies, and small bronze Greek-shaped pitchers and lamps, always antique, having been dug up by their veracious selves at Cuma and elsewhere. At Naples there is a regular factory of these modern antiques. Sold for what they are, they are worth any one's purchase; but these catiffs buy to re-sell them for what they are not.

Among the most appealing souvenirs were the cork models of the Greek temple at Paestum and other classical buildings. However, they were expensive. The Duke of Buckingham saw 'some cork models of the ancient ruins of the country' and passed them by: 'They are very beautiful, but ridiculously dear, so I bought none.'

A number of jewellers were producing archaeological-revival jewellery in the mid nineteenth century. Chief among them was Alessandro Castellani, who opened a workshop in 1863, and Casalta-Morabito, which made elaborate 'Pompeian-style' jewellery. Castellani's workshop was taken over by his manager, Giacinto Melillo, in 1870 and prospered into the twentieth century.

By 1862 it was possible to buy imitations of Etruscan vases from reputable dealers, and Murray's *Handbook* recommends Giustiniani and Colonnese.

Neapolitan foundries poured forth tens of thousands of copper alloy reproductions of items excavated at Pompeii and Herculaneum. The main manufacturers in the period 1860 to 1920 were Sabatino de Angelis, J Chiurazzi and G Sommer (who is perhaps better known today as a photographer). All three issued catalogues. Copies were available in different sizes and with different finishes, and there were marble and silver reproductions of certain items. The de Angelis and Chiurazzi firms combined in the early twentieth century.

Figure 25 shows a selection of reproductions of items excavated at Pompeii and Herculaneum, which were transferred to the National Museum of Naples. On the left are small bronzes acquired from Pasquale Scognamiglio in 1871. The copies of the *Dancing Faun* (found at Pompeii in 1831), the *Victory* and *Head of Brutus* were purchased from Sabatino de Angelis in 1888. All the silver on the right was bought from Sabatino de Angelis et fils in 1900.

25 *Reproductions of classical antiquities from Pompeii and Herculaneum, made in Naples between c1871 and 1900.*

Souvenirs with 'local colour' were provided by the makers of furniture decorated with marquetry at Sorrento (about sixteen miles south-east of Naples), who soon realised that they could sell small items to tourists.

Among the most common late nineteenth-century souvenirs are boxes, bowls and table-top music or book stands, decorated with peasants dancing or riding on donkeys (fig 26). One of the leading makers was Michele Grandville (1821-93), who labelled his wares. There was also a demand for painted terracotta or plaster figures of peasants. Murray's 1874 *Handbook* notes that Squadrilli also stocked 'the costume figures of the Calabrian and Sicilian peasantry from Castelgirone in the latter country'. These were made at Caltagirone in the south of Sicily, and may be signed (eg by members of the Bongiovanni and Vaccaro families).

It will be abundantly clear from all this that souvenirs were an integral part of the luxury goods industry in the eighteenth and nineteenth centuries. Their manufacture and sale employed large numbers of Italians and contributed to the general prosperity of all the major cities.

THE RISE OF THE URBAN SOUVENIR

BUILDINGS, BRIDGES AND COATS OF ARMS

Three-dimensional 'city souvenirs', as we understand them, are relatively rare before 1800. A great deal has obviously been destroyed, but the paucity of material also reflects a definite lack of activity in this area. Up until 1800, most makers concentrated on producing 'standard' good-quality or luxury goods and left the provision of 'city souvenirs' to print-makers and medal-lists. Any additional enterprise or energy tended to go into items celebrating contemporary figures or events, rather than into souvenirs showing towns, buildings or bridges – let alone civic coats of arms.

The production of city souvenirs was encouraged by the taste for paint-ings and prints of landscapes and townscapes in the eighteenth century, and by the closely related, developing vogue for *veduta* painting in porce-lain factories throughout Europe. This fashion for *vedute* naturally led to the depiction of local views on porcelain and earthenware in the late eigh-teenth century (fig 27) and reached a climax in the ceramics made at Vienna

27 Lidded cup and saucer by the Meissen porcelain facto-ry, near Dresden, painted in enamels with a view of Königstein Castle (seven-teen miles south-east of Dresden) and the river between Pobbart and Peternach. The bases of the pieces are painted with the mark used by Count Marcolini, the director of the factory, between 1775 and 1814.

and Berlin during the first half of the nineteenth century. Many of these are painted with local views intended to demonstrate the splendour of the capitals and the power and prestige of the Habsburg Empire and the Kingdom of Prussia. The pre-eminent pieces were generally commissioned for the courts or as official gifts, while other items were available to residents and the large numbers of visitors, as normal luxury goods or up-market souvenirs.

Some of the painters employed by, or associated with, the Vienna and Berlin factories also decorated glass that was included in lotteries or sold as souvenirs. In Vienna, Gottlob Samuel Mohn (1789-1825), Anton Kothgasser (1769-1851) and others painted glass beakers with views of St Stephen's Cathedral or the streets of Vienna. At Berlin, Carl von Scheidt (active 1812-21) enamelled beakers with the Brandenburg Gate and other scenes.

This top-quality work was very influential and galvanised many makers and merchants. The Bohemians were quick to see the potential and developed an extensive trade in souvenir glass, decorated with wheel-engraved views. Between about 1820 and 1850 they supplied many towns and cities in the German cultural area with first-rate beakers and other items. Agents succeeded in gaining orders from further afield, and consignments of red, green and yellow-flashed glasses were being sent to London, Edinburgh, York and other British cities in the mid nineteenth century.

The Russians were well aware of these developments and decorated more and more silver, ceramics and lacquer with *vedute*. After the Napoleonic Wars, Russian silversmiths began to produce large quantities of small silver rectangular boxes and other items decorated with niello (a black mix used to fill and emphasise engraved lines). Falconet's monument to Tsar Peter the Great in St Petersburg (unveiled in 1782) became the principal subject on snuff-boxes in the second quarter of the century (fig 28). The Kremlin and St Basil's Cathedral became increasingly popular and feature prominently on snuff-boxes, beakers, tea services, cigarette cases and caviar containers made in St Petersburg and Moscow between 1840 and 1890.

All these items were decorated by hand and were therefore comparatively expensive. What transformed the souvenir industry (as well as revolutionising the entire ceramic industry) was the introduction of transfer printing. Basically, this is a simple process. A design is engraved on a flat copper plate. The plate is coated with ink, wiped over, and a piece of damp tissue paper placed upon it. They are run through a heavy metal rolling press. The resulting print is then pressed, ink-side down, against the ware and rubbed to transfer the design. Once this has been done very thor-

oughly, the item is immersed in water to soften the paper and enable it to be removed with ease.

Ceramics can either be printed on the glaze or before it is applied – after the first 'biscuit' firing and prior to glazing and the second high-temperature firing. On-glaze printing only requires a low-temperature firing to 'fix' the decoration. Underglaze printing has the advantage that the decoration is protected by the glaze and is therefore less subject to wear. The disadvantage was that, until the 1830s, cobalt blue was usually the only colour that could withstand high-temperature firing.

Enamels and wood are transfer printed in the same way. Afterwards, the enamel has to be fired, at a low temperature, to bond the decoration. Wooden items might be given an additional coat of protective varnish.

The use of transfer printing made it possible to decorate items quickly and cheaply, and to supply a large percentage of the population with pieces they both wanted and could afford. Transfer printing was being used in England from the 1750s to decorate ceramics and enamels. The first important early transfer-printed souvenirs are the small oval 'patch-boxes' (with a mirror fitted inside the lid) which were made by enamellers in Bilston

28 Silver snuff-box with niello decoration representing Falconet's monument to Tsar Peter the Great, by the unidentified silversmith V.K, Moscow, 1826.

41

and other centres in South Staffordshire between about 1770 and 1820. They produced boxes for London, Bath, Brighton (Brighthelmstone), Tunbridge Wells, Buxton, Weymouth and other spas and seaside resorts (fig 29). Regrettably, only a few boxes can be associated with specific makers and it is seldom possible to attribute or date individual examples precisely.

These enamel boxes were followed, in the nineteenth century, by the Staffordshire potteries producing thousands of tons of earthenware transfer printed with thousands of different views of cities and towns in Britain and North America. The most highly acclaimed work was undertaken between about 1815 and the Copyright Act of 1842. Many of the views were copied from books of topographical illustrations, representing towns, churches, and the 'seats of the nobility and gentry'. Among the most active firms were Andrew Stevenson, Enoch Wood & Sons, J & R Clews and the Ridgways, who supplied both the domestic and North American markets. Figure 30 shows a typical example: a plate by J & W Ridgway, from their *Beauties of America* series. In this case, the source of the view is an engraving published in 1826, after a drawing by the Irish artist W G Wall, who went to America in 1818. Such ceramics were intended

primarily as part of an expensive dinner service, which would hopefully appeal to people in many towns and cities. However, they could also be sold as souvenirs in the town or city that they illustrated.

One of the most interesting makers of comparable 'blue and white' in Scotland was Watson's Pottery, at Prestonpans (to the east of Edinburgh), which was responsible for a punch bowl transfer printed with a splendid view of 'Edinburgh from Port Hopetoun', showing the Union Canal (opened in 1822) (fig 31). The transfer print is based on an engraving by W H Lizars, after a drawing by J Ewbank, published in *Picturesque Views of Edinburgh* in 1825. Between 1841 and 1851 J Jamieson & Co took on 'foreign' printers from England and trebled the workforce at the Bo'ness Pottery. This enabled them to make the *Modern Athens* dinner service, decorated

43

31 *Earthenware punch bowl transfer printed with a view of the canal basin at Port Hopetoun, Edinburgh, by Watson's Pottery, Prestonpans, c1825-30.*

with views of the Scott Monument and other sights in Edinburgh (fig 32). These pieces seem to have sold well, both under Jamieson & Co (to 1854) and John Marshall & Co (1854-99), and must have provided some excellent souvenirs of the 'Athens of the North'.

While these ceramics were being made, other firms were producing commemoratives and souvenirs celebrating achievements in contemporary civil engineering. The first such 'wonder' was the famous single-span Coalbrookdale Bridge, designed by the Shrewsbury architect Thomas

44

32 *Earthenware soup plate decorated with transfer prints of the Scott Monument and other 'modern' buildings in Edinburgh, by James Jamieson & Co, Bo'ness Pottery, Bo'ness, 1840s or early 1850s. The Scott Monument, designed by George Meikle Kemp, was begun in Princes Street Gardens in 1840 and John Steell's marble statue of Scott installed in the completed structure in 1846.*

Farnolls Pritchard and cast at Abraham Darby's Madeley Iron Works. It opened in 1779 and was soon represented on the lids of the small enamel boxes being made by the South Staffordshire enamellers, working to the east of Coalbrookdale.

Seventeen years later, the Coalbrookdale Bridge was overtaken by the 236-foot-long bridge across the River Wear at Sunderland (fig 33). This was built between 1792 and 1796 by Rowland Burdon, the MP for Sunderland and a partner in a bank at Berwick, and was regarded with great pride in the north-east. We can deduce that commemorative ceramics were being made in the early 1790s, because a view on a piece of creamware is captioned 'An East View of the Bridge *to be erected* across the River Wear' (author's italics). The views on many later ceramics are inscribed Moore & Co, the trading name of various ownerships and managements of the Wear Pottery, Southwick, from 1803. At least half a dozen local potteries made 'bridge ceramics', which were sold in the north-east – to residents, visitors and sailors – and also sent elsewhere in the UK and exported to Europe and North America (as part of the export trade in Sunderland ceramics). The large glass industry of the north-east also recognised that

33 *Earthenware and glass transfer printed or wheel-engraved with the Wearmouth Bridge. Both mugs contain ceramic frogs. The mug on the left is possibly by Dawson's Low Ford Pottery to the west of Sunderland, c1815-25, while that on the right is signed Moore & Co, Southwick, below the view, and probably dates from c1835-45. The jug is a product of the little-known but relatively prolific Low Lights Pottery in North Shields and is decorated with the characteristic colours and stylised ears of wheat used by the firm between c1826 and 1830. The goblet was made and engraved in Tyneside or Wearside, c1810-20.*

the Wearmouth Bridge could boost sales and wheel-engraved representations of it on goblets and rummers.

Marc Brunel's Thames Tunnel, linking Wapping and Rotherhithe, inspired an even wider range of souvenirs. Constructed between 1825 and 1843, the 1,200-foot-long road tunnel was an extremely difficult undertaking and wholly dependent upon Brunel's innovatory tunnelling shield. It was the Channel Tunnel of its day, and Victorians were thrilled by its successful completion. A million people walked through it within the first sixteen weeks of the official opening on 25 March 1843 (including 66,358 who attended the first of the great annual fairs in April). By the following March, a further million had paid the penny admission charge. As the tunnel became the greatest tourist attraction in London, the sixty-three open arches and forecourts were occupied by stalls selling food and souvenirs (fig 34).

Among the most noteworthy souvenirs are the various pull-out peepshows by Bondy Azulay, who ran counters 27, 41 and 62 in the tunnel, and the alabaster peep eggs containing small revolving views of the tunnel and other attractions, such as the Crystal Palace, which were noted by the American novelist Nathaniel Hawthorne in 1855. There are also transfer-printed plates, *papier-mâché* boxes and cases decorated with views of the tunnel, engraved horn beakers and shells, and many sewing aids, bearing inscriptions to the effect that they are 'A Present from the Thames Tunnel'.

46

Some items were definitely sold during the construction of the tunnel. However the majority must have been made in the 1840s and 1850s. By 1860 the tunnel had lost its glamour. Five years later it was purchased by the East London Railway Company, to serve as the Thames crossing for the line's trains.

The second half of the nineteenth century witnessed a steep rise in demand for comparatively inexpensive souvenirs, as the middle and working classes grew in number and in importance as consumers. They travelled in increasing numbers and had more and more money for opportunistic purchases. Manufacturers met (and stimulated) this appetite with new types of souvenirs. As we shall see, they generally reduced the size of the items and extended the use of transfer printing.

The earliest of the new wares were the varnished sycamore boxes and other items decorated with transfer prints, which were made by W & A Smith of Mauchline, Ayrshire (fig 35). These pieces have their origins in the snuff-boxes made by Charles Stiven at Laurencekirk, Kincardineshire, from the 1780s. Stiven was supported by the eccentric Lord Gardenstone, who persuaded Vincent Brixhe, a lacquermaster from Spa, to come to Laurencekirk around 1787. He was followed by H Henrard, who later returned to Spa.

Smith's apparently started in the early 1820s as makers of snuff-boxes and razor strops and were selling tartan-ware (objects decorated with

34 *Souvenirs of the Thames Tunnel, including an early peepshow by Azulay, an alabaster peep egg, and papier-mâché boxes and a cheroot case. The medal of Sir Marc Isambard Brunel is made of clay from the tunnel. A short history of the Thames Tunnel, probably written in the wake of the opening, mentions a 'handsome medal' of Brunel and notes: 'These are sold in the tunnel, as are several other articles, made principally from the clay taken out during the excavations'.*

35 *Wooden items decorated with transfer prints of Scottish buildings, with a steel plate engraved with views of London and Boulogne-sur-Mer used by W & A Smith of Mauchline. Printed inscriptions record that the small circular box showing Burns's Cottage was 'Bought in the Cottage', while the blotter with views of Stirling was 'Bought in the Douglas Room of the Royal Palace of Stirling'. Most of the pieces were probably made by Smith's. The circular box with a pincushion on the lid and a photograph of the National Gallery of Scotland on the side might be by the Caledonian Box Works.*

tartan patterns) by 1841. In 1850 they published *Authenticated Tartans of the Clans and Families of Scotland*, which publicised their method of 'machine painting' or printing tartan patterns. Smith's are known to have decorated a razor strop with a transfer print of the arms of King William IV (reigned 1832-37), but an account of a visit to their factory (published in the *Art Journal* in 1859) suggests that they were concentrating on tartan-ware and hand-painted boxes up until at least 1860.

Over the next seventy years Smith's produced huge quantities of boxes and table, desk and sewing accessories, decorated with transfer prints of local views, for British towns and cities, seaside resorts and exhibitions. They also exported similar items, decorated with appropriate views, to the Continent, India, Australia and North America. The factory remained in business until a fire in 1933.

Smith's were not the only manufacturers of transfer-printed wares. Alexander Brown, a former employee, founded the Caledonian Box Works at Lanark about 1866. Brown had a keen interest in photography, and it has been suggested that some of the 'Mauchline ware' decorated with photographs was made by his firm.

Cheap porcelain came to dominate the market in mass-produced souvenirs in the late nineteenth and early twentieth centuries. Colossal amounts were made in Germany and Bohemia, which had large porcelain industries and relatively low labour costs. On 1 February 1887 the *Pottery Gazette* alleged that wages were forty per cent lower in Germany and operatives were working twelve to sixteen hours a day. By 1 December the *Gazette* was complaining that German competition was severe and German ceramics were being sold at a lower price than they could be made in Britain.

There are many different types of German and Bohemian porcelain souvenirs (fig 36), but the most significant are the view-wares: items decorated with transfer-printed views of cities, towns and resorts. They are frequently enlivened with pink or blue enamel around the views and, sometimes, have pierced borders. The leading maker of plates with pierced borders was the Carl Schumann Porcelain Factory at Arzberg in Bavaria, which was responsible for the souvenirs of Blackpool and Ayr shown below. Founded in 1881, the firm generally employed a mark with a lion rampant on a shield, with 'Bavaria' above and 'Schumann' below.

Although many Continental pieces lack a maker's mark, the backstamp 'Made in Germany' (or Austria or Bohemia, etc) would suggest that they were made after the introduction of the British Merchandise Act of 1887

36 *German and Bohemian porcelain souvenirs for Ayr, Blackpool, the 1893 Columbian Exposition in Chicago, Coney Island, Edinburgh, Felixstowe, Oban, Perth and Scarborough, c1880-1939. The candlesticks are decorated with a view of Edinburgh Castle from the Grassmarket and are marked 'Manufactured in Germany'.*

or the American McKinley Tariff Act of 1891 (which made it mandatory to mark all imported items). Among the German and Bohemian manufacturers supplying the British market were the Mosanic Pottery of Max Emanuel & Co, Mitterteich, Bavaria (c1882-1918); the Victoria Porcelain Factory of Schmidt & Co of Altrohlau, Bohemia (1883-1945); and the Silesian Porcelain Factory of P Donath, Tiefenfurth, Silesia (1891-1916). Their most common marks are, respectively: three stacked rifles, various marks including the tradenames 'Victoria' or 'Gemma', and either a crowned S or crossed swords with an S. The backstamps on pieces for the American market refer to many other German, Bohemian and Austrian firms and often record the name of the importer (eg Wheelock or BFHS for Benjamin F Hunt & Sons) and the retailer.

British firms began to supply increasing quantities of ceramic viewwares to the United States from the 1890s. Josiah Wedgwood & Co made souvenir plates for the 1893 Columbian Exposition in Chicago and received an order from Jones, McDuffee, and Stratton Importing Company of Boston the same year for a series of blue plates decorated with views of Boston and the vicinity. The other key American importer

38 *Bust of W H Goss made by the Falcon Pottery after his death. The miniature mug and vase are decorated with transfer prints of Wells Cathedral and Shakespeare's House, Stratford-upon-Avon. Both are marked with a goshawk or falcon above 'W. H. GOSS' and date from between 1890 and 1930. The excellent models of Big Ben and St Paul's Cathedral are stamped with a similar mark, with 'ENGLAND' below. They were produced during H T Robinson's ownership of the factory, between 1930 and 1940. Other marks record that they were ordered by Selfridge's department store in London.*

was Rowland and Marsellus of New York, which began importing souvenir items about this time. Among the best-known British firms supplying the American market in the late nineteenth and early twentieth centuries were Wedgwood (which made over 1,500 different views), William Adams & Co and Doulton. Many of the views on the later British blue and white plates are based on photographs (fig 37).

These plates were aimed at collectors and did not satisfy the mass desire for cheap novelties. This craving was met by crested china: miniature pieces of porcelain decorated with coats of arms. Crested china became the most important type of souvenir in Britain between about 1900 and 1930, and employed hundreds of workers in Staffordshire and elsewhere.

The invention of crested china is credited to William Henry Goss (1833-1906), the owner of the Falcon Works, Stoke-on-Trent (fig 38). Writing after her father's death, Adeline Goss records that, in his early days, W H Goss produced ceramics decorated with coats of arms for 'the universities and some of the more noted public schools'. Later, apparently in the 1880s, he began to make small, slip-cast porcelain copies of ewers, jugs, urns and other artefacts which were associated with particular British towns. Many of these were based on sketches by his son Adolphus, who was the main traveller for the firm, securing orders from retailers. Adolphus also sketched and photographed views of towns and buildings which were used to decorate Goss's small view-wares. It seems that Adolphus was the real driving force behind the production of early crested china and the related view-ware souvenirs. Although Adolphus left the firm after his father's death, his brothers Victor and Huntley continued and expanded the business he had built up.

The Goss factory's miniature models were transfer printed in black with coats of arms, which could be coloured in by hand, and were sold through agents. Initially, it was intended that a model would only bear its associated coat of arms: thus a copy of the Aberdeen bronze pot would only be emblazoned with the arms of Aberdeen and would only be sold in the Granite City. But this was too restrictive, and it was soon possible to buy a wide range of items decorated with the arms of the agent's town. The number of Goss models went up from 136 in 1900 to 400 in 1921. In 1900 Goss had 481 British agents. Two years later there were 601, and 1,378 by 1921.

Crested china was taken up by many other Staffordshire potteries. Of these, the most significant were Arkinstall & Son Ltd, founded by Harold Taylor Robinson in 1903, and Wiltshaw & Robinson Ltd, which was established before 1890 and advertised 'Heraldic China' in 1902. Arkinstall items were made at the Arcadian Works in Stoke-on-Trent and marketed as Arcadian China. The Wiltshaw & Robinson pieces were produced at the Carlton Works, also in Stoke, and sold as Carlton Ware or Carlton China.

The main maker of crested china and related view-wares in Scotland was the Nautilus Porcelain Company, at the Possil Pottery in Glasgow (figs 39 and 40). This was run by MacDougall & Sons, the china, earthenware and glass merchants based at 77-79 Buchanan Street, Glasgow. They

39 *Porcelain view-wares by the Nautilus Porcelain Co, Glasgow. The pieces are transfer printed and over-painted in enamels with views of Abbotsford, Dunrobin Castle, Perth, St Andrews, Selkirk and Strathaven Castle.*

40 Opposite: *Crested china by the Nautilus Porcelain Co, Possil Pottery, Glasgow.*

Late eighteenth- and early nineteenth-century souvenirs would have been available in shops and also at circulating libraries. As Jane Austen observed in her unfinished novel *Sanditon*: 'The Library, of course, afforded everything; all the useless things in the world that could not have been done without.'

Brighton became the premier seaside resort in the nineteenth century. Its popularity was founded on its excellent position on the south coast, only forty miles from London, and on the patronage of the Prince Regent, later King George IV. The prince had been building and enlarging the 'Marine Pavilion' since 1787, but between 1815 and 1821 he transformed it into a fantastic palace, with 'Indian' domes and extravagant Oriental-style interiors. Smart society duly followed the prince to his favourite resort, drawing in their wake many much less exalted individuals and families.

The most significant souvenirs of Brighton between about 1800 and 1830 are the whitewood boxes decorated with coloured prints of the town (fig 44). Most of the early pieces would have been made at Tonbridge or

44 *Whitewood box and nutmeg grater decorated with coloured prints of the Chain Pier and Marine Parade and the Royal Pavilion, Brighton, c1825-40.*

Tunbridge Wells, just over thirty miles away. Trade labels and visual comparison reveal that the Tonbridge makers Thomas Wise (1750-1807) and his nephew and successor George Wise (1779-1869) were major producers. One of their boxes bears a view of Donaldson & Wilkes' Marine Library and suggests that their work was sold there. Fenner & Nye of Tunbridge published two prints of Brighton, dated March and April 1808, and presumably also supplied the Brighton market. In Brighton, the main early makers seem to have been the Morris family (from about 1814) and William Upton, who came from Tunbridge and was living at Brighton by 1815. A guide to Brighton in 1818 informs readers that: 'The manufacture of Tunbridge ware is becoming an object of importance here. The manufactories established are yet in their infancy, but are likely to receive a fair proportion of public encouragement.'

Among the other Brighton-based makers who published topographical prints of Brighton to decorate their wares are John Izard (from 1822), John Hunt, William Saunders and R Payne. Not surprisingly, the most common subjects are the Marine Parade with the Chain Pier in the background and the Royal Pavilion. The Wises and other makers in Kent and Sussex also supplied boxes for Margate, Hastings and other resorts in the south of England.

Visitors to Brighton were able to commission silhouettes. Many of these little paper or card portraits were cut, using scissors, in kiosks in the four archway towers of the Chain Pier, which was designed by Captain Samuel Brown and opened on 25 November 1823. This 1,154-foot-long structure was built as a landing point for the Brighton-Dieppe packets and for fashionable promenaders, who paid two pence for each admission or a guinea for the year. The Chain Pier developed into the first pleasure pier, with kiosks selling sweets, toys and refreshment. Telescopes were available, and a regimental band often played on the pier. At the base of the cliff, opposite the entrance, was a saloon and reading room with a library, and a bazaar. Other attractions included a camera obscura and a floating bath.

The first silhouettist, J Gapp (active c1827-40), was 'at the Third Tower in the centre of the Chain Pier', while Edward Haines (active late 1820s-c1896) was in the 'first left-hand Tower', according to his trade labels. Haines is listed in 'Tower 7' between 1848 and 1859, and may have moved to the 'Second Tower' after this. Both men charged 2s 6d for a full-length portrait and 1s for a bust. Although there were seventy-nine photographers in Brighton by 1871, silhouettes remained popular. The bearded French artist Huardel Bly was producing portraits to great acclaim in his

45 *Ornamental tray painted in enamels with Brighton from the sea by Chamberlain & Co, Worcester, c1840-45.*

kiosk on the West Pier until 1922. He was succeeded by Hubert Leslie, who carried on the tradition until 1939 and is reported to have cut 20,000 portraits.

The most impressive ceramic souvenirs would have been the ornamental trays, painted with a view of Brighton, by the Chamberlain porcelain factory at Worcester (fig 45). This type of tray was made in the early 1840s, with either a plain border or relief-moulded shells around the border. They were painted with various views, including Buckingham Palace, and sold for four guineas (£4 4s) with a plain border and five guineas (£5 5s) with moulded shell decoration. Unfortunately, it is not known how many Brighton trays were produced and whether sufficient were sold in Brighton for them to be regarded as stock souvenirs. Much more common and less problematic are the mid nineteenth-century Bohemian flashed glass goblets, beakers and other items, which are wheel-engraved with views of the Pavilion or the Chain Pier (fig 46). Some of the red-flashed glasses showing the Pavilion are either entirely or almost completely coated with red enamel, like the Bohemian glass souvenirs for

the 1851 Great Exhibition, and were probably made after the town decided to buy the redundant royal palace in 1849. The Pavilion finally became the property of the town commissioners in June 1850, when the public was admitted to the grounds, and the building itself was formally opened at a grand ball on 21 January 1851.

Brighton was for the élite and therefore exceptional – at least until the coming of the railway in 1841. This had the effect of turning on a hose. Whereas 117,000 had come to Brighton by road in 1835, 73,000 arrived by train in a single week in 1850. The expansion of the railway network, from 471 miles in 1835 to 30,843 miles in 1885, linked cities and towns with developing and potential seaside resorts. Railway travel made cheap day excursions and annual seaside holidays possible for most people. But it was a slow process. Although day excursions were already popular in the 1840s, weekend travel was severely restricted by the fact that most people worked on Saturdays and Sunday was widely, if not universally, regarded as 'the Lord's Day', and not a day for gallivanting off to the seaside.

The importance of the railways is reflected in the main group of mid nineteenth-century souvenirs: the earthenware mugs decorated with transfer prints of locomotives and carriages (fig 47). In an age of limited commercialisation, they were ideal souvenirs. Not only were they easy to make, but they could be sold to stockists in many towns. Retailers would have found them easy to order and relatively inexpensive. Above all, they appealed to the public and provided people with a splendid souvenir of what was probably the most exciting part of their excursion or holiday, if not a memento of the resort itself.

Many visitors to the seaside in this period were content to gather shells, pebbles, seaweed and other marine curiosities, either to keep as specimens or to use to make pattern-pictures or to decorate things. At some resorts they would have been able to buy locally-made items, decorated with shells and pebbles. At Whitby, on the Yorkshire coast, visitors could have availed themselves of the local speciality: jewellery and other articles carved from jet, washed ashore from an underwater seam.

Sir John Lubbock's Bank Holiday Act of 1871 was a great and lasting achievement. It added Boxing Day, Easter Monday, Whit Monday and the first Monday in August to the existing bank holidays, and enabled millions of people to spend the first Monday of August at the seaside, if they wished. The Holidays Extension Act of 1875 extended the 1871 Act to docks, customs houses, inland revenue offices and bonding warehouses, and consequently made it much easier for other businesses to observe the bank holidays.

47 *Earthenware mug transfer printed and over-painted in enamels with the 'Fury' pulling carriages, by John & Robert Godwin, Cobridge, Staffordshire, active 1834-66.*

The annual seaside holiday became feasible for most people as real wages rose and more and more employers allocated fixed annual leave with pay after about 1880. By the late nineteenth century the annual seaside holiday had spread to the lower middle class and better-off working classes. Blackpool was already attracting three million visitors a year in the 1890s. Forty years later, there were seven million a year and a further thirteen million were holidaying at six other major resorts: Southend (five-and-a-half million), Hastings (three million), Bournemouth and Southport (two million each), Eastbourne (over one million) and Ramsgate (one million).

The massive demand for souvenirs from all these people was partly met with Mauchline ware (fig 48), cheap German porcelain and crested china. All three were discussed in the previous chapter, but the crested china requires more attention here.

It is almost impossible to imagine the British seaside resorts without crested china. Millions of pieces were produced by Goss, Wiltshaw & Robinson, Arkinstall & Son and numerous British, German and Bohemian competitors. The predictable seaside souvenirs include copies of marine animals, shell dishes, bathing-machines, life-belts and lighthouses. At Blackpool there were various sizes of models of the Tower and Big Wheel, along with Lancashire clogs (fig 49). Miniature irons and teapots were presumably intended as humorous presents for

female relations. During World War I, British manufacturers produced a torrent of patriotic pieces: guns, tanks, aircraft, airships, ships, submarines, soldiers, nurses, ambulances, bullets, bombs, tents, sand-bags, caps, field-glasses – and this is certainly not a comprehensive list (fig 50). Later, there were models of war memorials. In the 1920s and 1930s the manufacturers and public understandably turned their backs on the horrors of the Great War and indulged themselves with cute, escapist, kitsch figures and animals. Some were modelled in the angular

49 Crested china decorated with the arms and motto of Blackpool by Arkinstall & Son Ltd (the bathing-machine) and Wiltshaw & Robinson Ltd (all the other pieces), Stoke-on-Trent, c1905-30.

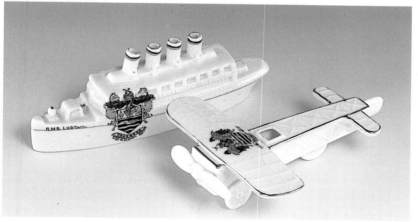

50 Porcelain models of the Cunard liner Lusitania, *sunk by German forces on 7 May 1915, and a 'Bleriot warplane', both decorated with the arms and motto of Blackpool. The ship was made by Wiltshaw & Robinson Ltd, the war-plane by Wileman & Co, Fenton, Longton, Staffordshire, c1915-25.*

51 *Earthenware by the
Longpark Pottery,
Torquay, c1920-57. The
milk jug, sugarbowl and
vase all have incised
inscriptions. The chamber
candlestick was painted
in pigment colours and
then glazed.*

and rounded forms of the new Art Deco style, and there was a clear pref-
erence for red and black, which provided the maximum contrast with
large areas of undecorated white porcelain.

Potteries at seaside resorts such as Torquay, Poole and Weston-super-
Mare also made ceramics for visitors. The Torquay potteries were particularly prolific (fig 51). Their main, 'bread and butter' products were small
decorative earthenware items inscribed with little sayings or other
mottoes. These were made between about 1900 and the 1950s-early 1960s
for resorts in the south-west of England and elsewhere in the UK.

'Motto ware', as it is called, is believed to have originated with pieces
made at the Aller Vale Pottery, between Torquay and Newton Abbot, in
the late nineteenth century. They had rhymes, precepts and quotations
scratched through the cream-coloured ground into the red clay body. Aller
Vale was taken over by Hexter, Humpherson & Co in 1897. Four years
later, Hexter's acquired the Watcombe Pottery at Torquay and began to
produce Aller Vale-type motto ware there. However, the decisive role in
the development of motto ware was played by the Brewer brothers, who
ran the Longpark Pottery, outside Torquay, between the late 1890s and
1905. They painted their tea services, mugs, jugs, tobacco barrels and other
items in slip (liquid clay) with a cockerel, cottage, fishing vessel or some
other subject, and incised a short motto above or alongside it. Their work

66

was copied and adapted by other Torquay potteries. Torquay pieces are often inscribed in the appropriate local dialect: thus an exaggerated Devon dialect for items intended for sale in the south-west and 'Scots' for those destined for Scotland. Some pieces are inscribed with the name of the resort. Motto ware with painted slip decoration continued to be made after slip decoration went out of general fashion in the 1910s. But firms responded to the change in taste. They began to paint old subjects, such as fishing vessels, in pigments (rather than in slip) and increased their range of lines with underglaze decoration. The two main makers of motto ware, Longpark and Watcombe, closed in 1957 and 1962 respectively.

These factory-made souvenirs were supplemented by the efforts of enterprising individuals, who cut silhouettes, blew and lamp-worked glass, took photographs in studios and on piers, and made many other things. Visitors could also operate the new money-in-the-slot machines to obtain souvenir 'eggs', press designs on coins or stamp names on strips of metal.

An even wider range of souvenirs was available at Coney Island and other American resorts. Although the Americans never developed a taste for British-style crested china, they had their own distinctive souvenirs, such as various types of glass and good quality die-struck souvenir spoons, and imported souvenirs from Japan well before the Europeans.

Coney Island is situated on Long Island, to the east of Manhattan and the south of Brooklyn. It used to be called 'the nation's playground', and its souvenirs (fig 52) can only be fully understood and appreciated in the context of its amazing history.

During the nineteenth century Coney Island developed to cater for the entire social and economic spectrum of New York and the East Coast. The wealthy stayed at three luxury hotels – the Manhattan Beach, Oriental and Brighton Beach – which were built between 1877 and 1880, to the east of what became the amusement park area. There they could enjoy good food and music by Sousa and other leading performers and bands. At the other extreme were the cheap bars, 'houses of ill repute' and 'dens of iniquity' in 'The Gut' and on 'The Bowery', which earned Coney the sobriquet of 'Sodom by the Sea'. A major attraction for all classes was the horse-racing at the three race-tracks: Brighton Beach, Sheepshead Bay and Gravesend. They opened in 1879, 1880 and 1886 respectively and made Coney the race-track capital of America. Brighton Beach closed in 1907, and the enforcement of anti-gambling legislation resulted in the closure of the other two tracks in 1910.

Five million people are said to have visited Coney in 1882 and to have spent nine million dollars there. Two years later, Lamarcus Thompson pioneered Coney's mechanised ride business when he built the first amusement railway in the world, the Switchback Railroad. In 1897 George C Tilyou opened one of the first enclosed amusement parks, Steeplechase Park (named after its star attraction, a mechanised horse-race). It was followed by Frederic Thompson and Elmer Dundy's Luna Park (to the north-east of Steeplechase) in 1903 and by Dreamland (to the east of Steeplechase) in 1904. These parks had mechanised rides, spectacular architecture, and many other attractions. Luna claimed to be lit by 250,000 electric light bulbs, while Dreamland boasted a million. Four million people visited Luna in 1904. Steeplechase burned down in 1907 but was quickly rebuilt. Dreamland suffered the same fate in 1911 and was not replaced.

The extension of the subway to Coney in 1920 led to a sharp rise in visitors and a reduction in prices. The recession of the late 1920s-early 1930s caused great difficulties, and Luna went bankrupt in 1933. Nevertheless, over sixteen million people came to Coney each summer in the 1930s. Most of Luna went up in flames in 1944 and 1946, and subsequently became a housing development. Coney continued to be popular after World War II – with one and a half million basking in the sun one sweltering day in 1952 – but the magic was gone. Steeplechase finally closed in 1964-5 'for lack of business'.

Large quantities of moulded glass beakers, drinking glasses and jugs, imitating cut glass, were on sale at Coney between about 1900 and 1914. The most common surviving pieces are made of colourless glass and decorated with a deep band of red flashing. Identical or almost identical glasses were sold in connection with the 1904 St Louis Exposition and other American exhibitions of the period. Other items are made in light, translucent green glass and enriched with a narrow band of gilding, which gives them a distinctly 'classy' appearance but soon wears off. Both types of glass are frequently found with wheel-engraved inscriptions, which are often dated. A more sophisticated and expensive range of colourless glass was blown or pressed in very good-quality moulds, partly flashed with red enamel, and then inscribed, painted with flowers and gilded.

German porcelain was also available in abundance. The best pieces were probably the view-ware plates with pierced borders by Schumann of Arzberg and other German firms. But the volume sales were of small ornamental vases and other items with printed views 'reserved' against a deep blue ground. These are generally only marked 'Made in Germany'. Comparable pieces with a deep blue ground were made for British towns and resorts, but were much more popular in the United States. Various souvenirs record the magical, and to contemporaries almost miraculous,

52 *Souvenirs of Coney Island made in Bohemia, Germany, the United States and Japan, c1880-1965. The plate at the back is printed with a view of the Manhattan Beach Hotel and the Oriental Hotel on Manhattan Beach, and is impressed with the mark 'Carl Knoll/CARLSBAD' used by the Karlsbad Porcelain Factory of Carl Knoll at Fischern, Bohemia, in the nineteenth century.*

68

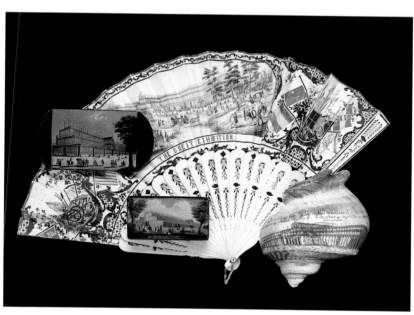

54 Red-flashed glass vases and goblets wheel-engraved with views of the Crystal Palace, Bohemian, c1851. The goblet on the right is inscribed 'THE CRYSTAL PALACE/ OR/ MONSTER BUILDING FOR THE GRAND INTERNATIONAL EXHIBITION OF 1851'.

55 Fan, engraved shell, and papier-mâché box and cheroot case decorated with views of the Crystal Palace, c1851. The shell is signed 'C. H. Wood. Pearl engraver to the Queen'.

73

56 *British ceramic souvenirs of the 1851 Great Exhibition. The porcelain and the earthenware vase on the left are marked 'GREEN/LONDON'. John & Robert Godwin of Cobridge made the earthenware mugs and jug, while J & M P Bell & Co of Glasgow was responsible for the plate.*

Specialist souvenir sellers were well established by the 1880s, and the new department stores became significant outlets.

The early ceramics merit particular attention. Heading the field are the earthenware vases and porcelain tea and coffee wares marked 'GREEN/LONDON', which are decorated with transfer prints of the Crystal Palace from Hyde Park Corner and the interior of the building. These views were registered to the ceramic retailer James Green of 35-36 Upper Thames Street, London, by the Patent Office on 20 January 1851, under design numbers 75883 and 75884. Only a few paces behind are the earthenware mugs and jugs transfer printed in blue with views of the Crystal Palace. The 'J. & R.G.' on the bases of most examples stand for the Staffordshire potters John & Robert Godwin of Sneyd Green, Cobridge. Bell's of Glasgow also made earthenware plates, transfer printed with views of the exterior of the 1851 building, which probably qualify as souvenirs.

British and Continental factories made huge quantities of ceramics for the later exhibitions. Among the most interesting are the British pieces for the American market. Wedgwood's produced pitchers, with moulded decoration and printed views of Memorial Hall and Independence Hall, for the 1876 Philadelphia Exhibition and plates showing views of exhibition buildings for the 1893 Columbian Exposition in Chicago. Adams & Co and other British firms sent plates for the 1904 St Louis Exposition. Nearer to home, Bell's made fine plates and jugs for the 1888 and 1901 Glasgow Exhibitions. On the Continent, Franz Anton Mehlem of Bonn manufactured transfer-printed plates with a well-designed composition of five views and a bust of Queen Victoria for the 1887 Manchester Exhibition, while the little-known French firm of Sarreguemines produced imaginatively designed sets of transfer-printed plates for the 1889 Paris Exposition. All of these are good-quality, relatively expensive pieces, and it was left largely to anonymous German manufacturers to supply the bottom half, or more, of the market with small cups, vases and other items. These vary in quality, but are often crudely made and decorated, and were clearly intended to sell for very little.

The Bohemians supplied impressive wheel-engraved red-flashed vases and goblets for the 1851 Exhibition, but seem to have sent small, much less distinguished items for the International Exhibition in London eleven years later. They were superseded by the acid-etchers, led by the Compagnie des Cristalleries de Saint-Louis, at Saint-Louis lès-Bitche in Lorraine. This famous firm was acid-etching glass in the 1860s and appears to have made a special effort for the 1889 Paris Exposition, after which it

57 Amber-stained and clear glass souvenirs by Saint-Louis for the 1889 Universal Exposition in Paris, the 1890 International Exhibition in Edinburgh and the 1892 Isle of Man Exhibition. The other side of the Edinburgh tumbler shows the Forth Bridge, which was declared open by the Prince of Wales on 4 March 1890.

used its capacity to supply other exhibition centres, including Edinburgh and the Isle of Man in 1890 and 1892 (fig 57). Its glass beakers are normally either clear or amber-stained and signed 'S^T LOUIS' and 'Made in Lorraine'.

Some of the most interesting exhibition souvenirs were made at or near the exhibitions. They stem from manufacturers wanting to show their machinery or processes in operation. Such displays were very popular with the public, and exhibition organisers provided power to the machinery halls and allowed exhibitors to sell the items that they made, or decorated, on their stands.

At the 1851 Exhibition, Applegarth's vertical printing machine was used to print exhibition supplements of the *Illustrated London News*, thus setting the precedent for hundreds of later printing and newspaper displays. The production of commemorative medals at exhibitions also goes back a long way. Pinches & Co of London and Uhlhorn of Grevenbroich, in Germany, both seem to have had static displays at the 1851 Exhibition. However, Pinches was definitely striking medals at the Crystal Palace shortly after it reopened at Sydenham, in south London, in 1854, and both firms were mass-producing medals at the 1862 Exhibition, to the delight of visitors.

Enormous quantities of 'normal' textiles and souvenir textiles must have been made at exhibitions between 1860 and 1914. The most remarkable are the book-markers, pictures and other items woven on Jacquard looms, generally erected in the machinery-in-motion sections of exhibitions. They were invented by Thomas Stevens of Coventry, whose early work includes book-markers woven at the 1866 York Exhibition, which refer directly to the exhibition. Stevens went on to take part in the 1873 Vienna and 1876 Philadelphia Exhibitions. At Philadelphia he produced 'Centennial' book-markers decorated with President Washington and was praised for having 'the finest loom'.

Stevens' first silk pictures are believed to be the four York-related designs woven at the 1879 York Exhibition. He followed these with many more and installed looms at exhibitions in Edinburgh, Manchester, Newcastle and Glasgow between 1886 and 1888, which produced views of the exhibition buildings and the 'Old Edinburgh Street' at the 1886 Edinburgh Exhibition.

After his death in October 1888, his sons Thomas and Henry continued the Stevengraph Works. They introduced many more subjects and set up looms at the Edinburgh and Glasgow Exhibitions in 1890 and 1901. Between these dates they also invested heavily in the 1893 Chicago Exposition, sending looms and men who turned out book-markers of

LANDING OF COLUMBUS. OCT 12 1492

Columbus and the *Santa Maria*, pictures of Columbus leaving Spain and landing in America, and other special lines (fig 58).

Stevens' chief British competitor was William Henry Grant (1858-1931), who founded W H Grant & Co of Coventry in the early 1880s. Grant's operated looms at the 1886 and 1908 Edinburgh Exhibitions and concentrated on producing good views of exhibitions, which made ideal souvenirs. In the United States the Phoenix Silk Manufacturing Co wove first-rate book-markers at the 1876 Philadelphia and 1893 Chicago Exhibitions, and was challenged by John Best & Co. Both firms were based in the main American silk-manufacturing centre of Paterson, New Jersey (about fourteen miles from New York City).

Glass-makers and decorators also seized the opportunity to promote themselves and sell items at exhibitions. Gillinder & Sons of Philadelphia (founded in 1861) paid $3,000 for the concession and built a glassworks in the grounds of the 1876 Philadelphia Exhibition. In *The Centennial Exhibition Described and Illustrated*, J S Ingram records:

> The whole process of manufacturing glass was here shown, and it was a very interesting and highly instructive exhibit. Many of the articles manufactured were especially designed as mementos of the great exhibition, and found a ready market. These included paper weights, upon which were stamped representations of different Centennial buildings, or public buildings of the city; busts of Washington, Lincoln and others, vases, colored ornaments and trinkets.

Another account lists 'very pretty little glass slippers, paper-weights of different kinds, delicate wine glasses and tumblers, flower-holders, pitchers and other pleasing souvenirs'. Most of these pieces were press-moulded, generally in colourless glass, although white glass was also used

58 *Silk picture of the 'Landing of Columbus' on October 12 1492, by Thomas Stevens of Coventry. This was probably first issued at the 1893 Chicago Exposition. Many examples bear the printed inscription 'WOVEN IN PURE SILK AT THE WORLD'S COLUMBIAN EXPOSITION, CHICAGO, 1893.' on their card-mounts.*

for some of the busts and other ornaments. Many have an acid-etched, 'frosted' finish. The paperweights are generally unmarked, but the busts and other ornaments are frequently signed 'CENTENNIAL EXHIBITION GILLINDER & SONS', either on the bases or backs (fig 59). The exhibition attracted nearly ten million visitors, and Gillinder's must have made money and benefited from the publicity.

Temporary glassworks were constructed at many later exhibitions, including Paris, Edinburgh and Pittsburgh in 1889, 1890 and 1891. But the most important, as far as souvenirs are concerned, are the glasshouses built by the Libbey Glass Co of Toledo, Ohio, and the Venice and Murano Glass Co in the Midway Plaisance amusement area to the west of the World's Columbian Exposition in Chicago in 1893, which drew at least 27.5 million visitors. The Libbey factory was a substantial building, in which every aspect of glass-making and decorating could be seen. At first, there was no charge and the building was swamped with visitors, provoking complaints from neighbouring amusement operators. A ten-cent admission charge was levied from 15 May, which roughly halved the crowds to a manageable 18,700 a week. The price was increased to twenty-five cents in the final month. Over two million are said to have toured the factory, netting Libbey's a handsome profit from admissions and sales. Among the obvious souvenirs are press-moulded paperweights in the form of a woman's head and a hatchet decorated with a bust of President Washington, and paperweights printed with photographic views of the

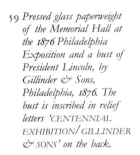

59 *Pressed glass paperweight of the Memorial Hall at the 1876 Philadelphia Exposition and a bust of President Lincoln, by Gillinder & Sons, Philadelphia, 1876. The bust is inscribed in relief letters 'CENTENNIAL EXHIBITION/ GILLINDER & SONS' on the back.*

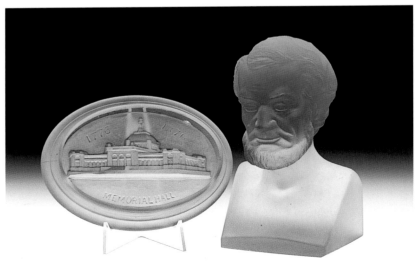

exposition (fig 60). All are marked as Libbey products and refer to the exposition, and some actually state that they were made at the fair by Libbey's.

In 1908 Thomas Webb & Sons of Stourbridge responded by erecting a glassworks at the Franco-British Exhibition at Shepherd's Bush in London. The admission charge was sixpence and the 150,000 visitors were able to buy small glass pigs and other items in souvenir boxes (fig 61).

60 *Pressed glass hatchet deco-rated with a bust of President Washington and a paperweight showing the Massachusetts State Building at the 1893 Columbian Exposition, by the Libbey Glass Co, Toledo, Ohio, 1893. The other side of the hatchet-blade is inscribed 'WORLD'S.FAIR./1893.'*

61 *Souvenir from Thomas Webb & Sons' glassworks at the 1908 Franco-British Exhibition.*

62 *Tumbler with sand-blasted decoration and signed base by John Ford & Co, Edinburgh, and a child's mug by Sowerby's of Gateshead, with sand-blasted decoration attributed to Ford's, c1886.*

During this period, visitors to Scottish exhibitions were able to purchase good glass souvenirs by John Ford & Co's Holyrood Glass Works, based in Edinburgh, and John Baird of Port Dundas, Glasgow. In addition to their static display of finished goods, Ford's had another stand at the 1886 Edinburgh Exhibition, in the machinery-in-motion section, which demonstrated the processes of glass-blowing, cutting and engraving. Here glass pipes, model ships and artificial birds were fashioned using a gas blowlamp, and names quickly engraved on children's mugs. 'A novelty on this stand' (to quote the *Official Guide* to the exhibition) was 'the sand-blast machine for glass ornamentation'. According to the *Official Catalogue* and *Guide*, Ford's operated this stand 'in conjunction with Tilghman's Patent Sand-blast Machine Company, Bellefield Works, Sheffield', and had set up a steam-powered Mathewson's Patent Sand-blast Machine. Benjamin Chew Tilghman's process for sand-blasting was patented in London in 1870 and shown at the 1873 Vienna Exhibition. Glass could be partly protected from the hail of particles by paper stencils, 'paint' applied by block printing, or a photographic film of bichromatised gelatine. Jeremiah Eugene Mathewson's improvements to the apparatus were patented in 1884. Ford's used the Mathewson machine to sand-blast souvenirs with an oval view of 'The Netherport & French Ambassador's House' in the 'Old Edinburgh Street' at the exhibition and sand-blasted the bases with the inscription 'J. FORD & C°', surrounded by 'PATENT SAND

BLAST·EDINBRO· (fig 62). The same view is also found on press-moulded children's mugs bearing the peacock mark of Sowerby's Ellison Glass Co Ltd, of Gateshead, on their bases. These and other related items are believed to have been sand-blasted by Ford's.

Although Ford's won a bronze medal for the sand-blast machine at the 1886 Exhibition, it was John Baird (later John Baird Ltd) who became the main producer of glass souvenirs and advertising glass in Scotland. Baird had shown a static display of glass at the 1886 Exhibition and seems to have been profoundly impressed by Ford's activities. At the 1888 Glasgow Exhibition, he mounted a static display in the Main Building and a demonstration of 'Glass Engraving and Decorating by [the] Sand Blast Process' in the machinery section. This was followed by static and demonstration displays, involving sand-blasting, acid-etching, printing and enamelling, at the Edinburgh and Glasgow Exhibitions of 1890, 1901, 1908 and 1911. Unfortunately, Baird's only marked their items for the Scottish National Exhibition held in Edinburgh in 1908 (fig 63). They are signed 'JOHN BAIRD, L.ᵀᴰ, GLASGOW' (or similar). Many of these signed pieces are simply inscribed 'A/Present from/SCOTTISH NATIONAL/EXHIBITION/Edinburgh 1908', with 'SCOTTISH NATIONAL/EXHIBITION' on a decorated scroll. The arms of Scotland appear above the inscription on some items, and some also have a bust of King Edward VII on the opposite side. Other signed pieces are decorated with views of the exhibition buildings, Holyrood

63 *Glass souvenirs by John Baird Ltd, Glasgow, for the Scottish National Exhibition in Edinburgh in 1908. All five pieces are signed directly below the decoration and inscriptions.*

81

64 *Glass souvenirs for the 1901 Glasgow International Exhibition, attributed to John Baird Ltd. All three show James Miller's temporary Industrial Hall, to the east of the new Kelvingrove Art Gallery and Museum.*

65 *Glass souvenirs for the Scottish Exhibition of National History, Art and Industry, held in Glasgow in 1911, attributed to John Baird Ltd. The large tumbler and jug are decorated with the Stewart Memorial Fountain, which was almost in the centre of the exhibition in Kelvingrove Park.*

Palace or Edinburgh Castle. These items enable glass souvenirs for the 1901 and 1911 Glasgow Exhibitions, with comparable 'A Present from' inscriptions and other characteristics, to be attributed to Baird's. The main group of 1901 souvenirs has a view of the Industrial Hall above the inscription 'GLASGOW INTERNATIONAL EXHIBITION 1901' (fig 64), while the 1911 glass often shows the Stewart Fountain above 'STEWART FOUNTAIN/SCOTTISH EXHIBITION, GLASGOW, 1911/PALACE OF HISTORY' on a scroll (fig 65).

Many souvenirs reflect the increasing emphasis upon entertainment at exhibitions. This goes back to the 1867 Paris Exhibition, when the building was surrounded by a park packed with dozens of features and side-shows, including a Russian village and reconstructions of Egyptian and Mexican temples. At the 1873 Vienna Exhibition visitors were able to enjoy a Japanese village and the amusements in the Prater. In 1884 the organisers of the International Health Exhibition, held at South Kensington, erected a 'Street in Old London', at a cost of £6,000. It was much admired and

66 *Souvenirs of the 1886 Edinburgh Exhibition. The earthenware mug and vase are by D Methven & Sons and are transfer printed with a view of the exhibition building in the Meadows and two views of the 'Old Edinburgh Street'. Hautin & Boulanger made the plate, which shows the Netherport and French Ambassador's House in the Street. The wooden box is transfer printed with the exhibition building and the Royal Porch in the Street and is attributed to W & A Smith, who took part in the exhibition.*

inspired a number of other reconstructions, including the 'Old Edinburgh Street' at the 1886 Edinburgh Exhibition, which was built for £4,000.

The 'Old Edinburgh Street', composed of replicas of demolished buildings, is represented on glass tumblers and mugs, silk pictures by Thomas Stevens and W H Grant & Co, Mauchline boxes, and ceramics by D Methven & Sons' Kirkcaldy Pottery, Moore & Co, Hautin & Boulanger of Choisy-le-Roi, near Paris, and others (fig 66). Moreover, many of these items were actually sold in the street, for the exhibition organisers rented out the ground-floor rooms as shops, for between £20 and £80, and required staff to wear period costume. W H Grant had a working loom at number 11 (as well as the looms in the exhibition itself). P Macgregor Westren sold his exhibition medals at number 14. David Anderson and Richard Sprengel, the souvenir sellers in the Arcade, Princes Street, were at numbers 4 and 13 respectively, while Henry Begg, one of the leading souvenir specialists in Edinburgh in the late nineteenth-early twentieth centuries, was at number 28. Begg advertised in the exhibition catalogue:

STRANGER!

Dinna leave AULD EDINBURGH withoot takin' a Keek at

No. 28 Ye Heart o' Midlothian Boothe,

whaur Jeanie and Effie Deans sall serve ye richt blithely wi' fouth o' braw Knick-Knacks an' bonnie Keepsakes o' ye Exhibition.   HENRY BEGG, ye Laird.

Reconstructions continued to be popular well into the twentieth century. A reconstruction of the Bishop's Palace at the 1888 Glasgow Exhibition (which is represented on earthenware mugs) was followed by the 'Auld Toon' at the 1911 Glasgow Exhibition. In turn, the Highland Village at the 1911 Exhibition was repeated at the 1938 Glasgow Empire Exhibition, and represented on souvenirs made by Goss and others.

Many souvenirs also relate to the amusements at or alongside exhibitions. A large and diverse group represent the original Ferris Wheel at the 1893 Chicago Exposition and its successors at Earl's Court, London, and the 1900 Paris Exposition (fig 67). The re-erection of the Chicago Wheel at the 1904 St Louis Exposition led to yet more souvenirs.

Exhibition souvenirs show considerable continuity. At the same time, many twentieth-century items reflect new manufacturing technologies and changes in society. The most obvious difference is the decrease in size, which reduced prices and increased the number of potential purchasers.

Among the early examples are the 'Grafton' miniatures, made by A B Jones & Sons Ltd of Longton, Staffordshire, for the 1908 Franco-British Exhibition and the later exhibitions at the White City (fig 68).

New materials have increased variety. Aluminium was a rare and expensive metal in the mid nineteenth century, used for jewellery and the cutlery for the Emperor Napoleon III, but the discovery of commercial manufacturing processes resulted in plentiful, cheap supply. In the United

67 *Bronze medal and coloured photograph showing the Ferris Wheel at the 1893 Chicago Exposition, with the Big Wheel at Earl's Court represented on a nickel-plated iron tray of 1896, and a tin-plated iron 'Souvenir l'Exposition Paris 1900'.*

68 Earthenware vase and plate for the 1908 Franco-British Exhibition by W Adams & Co, Tunstall, Staffordshire, with 'Grafton' miniature porcelain by Alfred B Jones & Sons Ltd, Grafton China Works, Longton, Staffordshire. The 'Grafton' china is for the 1908 Franco-British Exhibition (left), the 1912 Latin-British Exhibition (centre) and the 1914 Anglo-American Exhibition (right). All three exhibitions were held at the White City, London.

69 Aluminium souvenirs of the Pan-American Exposition, Buffalo, 1901 and the Louisiana Purchase Exposition, St Louis, 1904. The box with a beautiful tight-fitting lid and four technically perfect medals showing buildings at the St Louis Exposition are by the Schwaab Stamp & Seal Co, Milwaukee.

States, output went up from about eighty pounds in 1883 to seven-and-a-half million pounds in 1893, while the cost plummeted from thirty-two dollars to fifty cents a pound. This had an almost immediate effect on exhibition souvenirs, with more and more aluminium items being produced for the 1893 Chicago, 1901 Buffalo and 1904 St Louis Exhibitions (fig. 69).

Plastics and chrome-plating have subsequently become even more important. Cellulose nitrate (celluloid) and phenol formaldehyde (Bakelite) have been available since the mid nineteenth century and 1907 respectively. They were used for small souvenirs, such as badges and napkin rings, in the early twentieth century, but really made a major impact, along with cellulose acetate, in the 1930s. Since then, they have been joined by melamine, polyethylene, polystyrene and nylon. Chrome-plated souvenirs have received scant attention, partly because they are often unmarked. The shapes of the trays in figure 70 were registered to Samuel Groves & Co Ltd, Musgrave Works, Hockley, Birmingham, in 1933 and 1934, as design numbers 780517 and 789649, and suggest that this firm warrants further investigation.

A less obvious development is the appearance of bigger, better and more imaginative advertising souvenirs, either for sale or distribution as

70 *Plastic, chrome-plated and aluminium souvenirs for the 1938 Empire Exhibition in Glasgow. The 1/60-scale plastic models of Thomas Tait's Tower of Empire are by Lanarkite Ltd, Newarthill, near Motherwell, which manufactured door furniture, ship and bathroom fittings and advertising novelties. The bottle-opener and boxed 'novelties' on the right were made of the British Aluminium Company's BA/35 Alloy by M C L and Repetition Ltd, Birmingham.*

71 *Lipton souvenirs for the British Empire Exhibitions held at Wembley in 1924 and 1925.*

72 *Souvenir mirror by the Pittsburgh Plate Glass Co from the Glass Center at the 1939 New York World's Fair. The printed rayon handerkerchief or scarf was acquired elsewhere.*

free gifts. The classic British examples are the brass tea caddies and aluminium chocolate boxes and preserve-jar containers which Lipton's, the tea manufacturers, sold at the 1924 and 1925 British Empire Exhibitions at Wembley (fig 71). It is worth noting, for the benefit of owners, that the designs for the 1925 brass tea caddies were registered to Samuel Heath & Sons Ltd, Cobden Works, Birmingham, as 711485 and 711486, on 4 March 1925.

At the 1939 New York World's Fair, the Pittsburgh Plate Glass Co installed the largest mirrored ceiling in the world in the Glass Building, and neatly complemented this by handing out small boxed mirrors (fig 72). Other items have been sold at a discount to encourage people to buy a particular product. The purchaser of seven bars of Ogston's XX pale soap could acquire a set of seven Sheffield electroplated fruit spoons, decorated with the 1938 Glasgow Empire Exhibition lion and valued at 10 shillings, for only 1s 9d!

In retrospect, the key development between the two World Wars was the general agreement to decorate exhibition souvenirs with the exhibition symbol or principal architectural feature, or both. J C Herrick's design of a standing lion for the 1924 British Empire Exhibition was reproduced on many souvenirs for the 1924 and 1925 Empire Exhibitions. Thirteen years later, the hatched rampant lion of the 1938 Glasgow Exhibition was even more in evidence on the souvenirs, and many also represent Thomas Tait's landmark Tower of Empire. The 1939 New York World's Fair endorsed this movement and provided the model for later exhibitions. At the centre of the 1939 fair, the organisers constructed the 700-foot-high Trylon and Perisphere and adopted them as the official exhibition logo. Most souvenirs depict or echo this superb, inspiring feature and many also bear the symbol of a conjoined triangle-circle. The success of the Trylon and Perisphere and the souvenirs led to the Atomium at the 1958 Brussels Expo, the Space Needle at the 1962 Seattle World's Fair and the Unisphere at the 1964-5 New York World's Fair and their related souvenirs.

Some of the best twentieth-century souvenirs were made for the 1939-40 New York Fair (fig 73). They include the ceramics by Lenox, Inc, Trenton, New Jersey (to designs attributed to the chief designer Frank Graham Holmes and the chief modeller Ernest Henk), the Homer Laughlin China Co, Newell, West Virginia (designed by Charles Murphy) and the Cronin China Co, Minerva, Ohio. Among the outstanding plastic souvenirs are the salt and pepper shaker in the shape of the Trylon and Perisphere by the Emeloid Co, Arlington, New Jersey, and the Trylon-Perisphere puzzle by the Helenhart Novelty Corp, New York, which are

73 Overleaf: *Souvenirs of the 1939-40 New York World's Fair. The three earthenware plates are by (from left to right): W Adams of Staffordshire (for Tiffany & Co), the Cronin China Co, and Homer Laughlin. Both vases are by Lenox, Inc. The glass tumbler with the red printed decoration is by Libbey's, while the dish on the left is a very fine example of 'SyrocoWood', which was made by the Syracuse Ornamental Co in Syracuse, New York.*

89

both made of cellulose acetate and cellulose nitrate. Exhibition colours had been used before, but the 1939 Board of Design employed them with flair and discipline. Many souvenirs and packaging are decorated with the exhibition colours white, orange-red and blue, and the licence numbers indicate the very firm control over merchandising by the Executive Committee of the Board of Directors and others working for the fair.

The Japanese made many metal and ceramic souvenirs for the 1933-4 Chicago Exhibition and the 1939-40 New York Fair (fig 74). They subsequently supplied a high percentage of the metal models of the Space Needle for the 1962 Seattle Fair and the lightweight metal dishes and other items for the 1964-5 New York World's Fair.

MODERN MEMENTOES IN A SHRINKING WORLD

Over the past thirty years the increasing prosperity of most people in the developed countries and greater leisure time have led to an astronomic rise in mass travel – by road, rail, air and sea. The stage has now been reached when over a billion well-off domestic and international travellers and tourists are visiting cities, beaches, theme parks and a myriad of other tourist attractions each year, and are able and willing to buy all manner of mementoes.

Tourism has become the world's largest industry, with an estimated value of $3.4 trillion in 1995 and predicted growth to $7.2 trillion by 2005. At the same time, there has also been enormous expansion in the related leisure, sports and heritage sectors and a growing emphasis upon commercialisation and selling souvenirs and other products.

Souvenir and gift shops abound – even in museums, cathedrals and universities. Some idea of the proliferation of souvenirs is revealed by glancing at just one of the less well-known English cathedrals. At Peterborough, for instance, you can buy Peterborough Cathedral wine; engraved cut glass decanters; dusters, oven gloves, T-shirts and tea towels, all bearing the cathedral's picture; or teddy bears, 'found at Peterborough Cathedral'. There is even a Cathedral and Church Shops Association, with an annual 'Cathedral Show', attended by about fifty traders and a hundred shop managers.

All the indications are that the huge boom in the number and diversity of souvenirs over the past fifty years will continue.

One of the two most fundamental developments in recent years has been the placing of more and more orders in the Far East. As we saw in the last two chapters, Japan was a major supplier of souvenirs between about 1930 and 1965. After this, it became more profitable to do business with Taiwan and Singapore. Now, the improvement of international relations between America and China and very low labour costs have transformed the People's Republic of China into the workshop of the world, with other orders being met by firms in Taiwan and South Korea. The pace of change has been spurred on by economic recessions, which have made people much more cautious about spending their money and have

increased the pressure on suppliers and retailers to buy and sell as cheaply as possible. Recently, it has gained added momentum as the Western economies and currencies have strengthened and the so-called 'tiger economies' of Asia have collapsed.

The model of the Statue of Liberty on the left of figure 75 illustrates just how cheaply items can be manufactured in China. It was possible for the factory, various transporters, the importer – City Merchandise Inc, Brooklyn – and the retailer in Times Square, New York, all to make money without pushing the retail price above $2.99. By contrast, the admittedly better-quality, American-made model to the right, by Colbar Art Inc, costs $14.99. The Chinese mug and South Korean plate shown alongside demonstrate the high standard of Asian porcelain and colour printing. Produced for Harvey Hutter & Co Inc, they sell for only $6.99 and $10.99 respectively at the same shop in Times Square.

It is obviously extremely difficult for many Western manufacturers of ceramics, plastics, textiles and enamels to compete with cheap, first-rate souvenirs from China and other Asian countries. They need to cut costs, which generally means shedding labour, and, whenever possible, introduce sophisticated machinery that combines high-volume output with the flexibility of producing short runs of items. An excellent example is the

80 *Light shade hand-painted with coloured sands by Navajo Indians, Sunwest Indian Art, Ltd, c1992. Shown with part of a cotton hanging printed with a design by an Aboriginal artist, Karen L Taylor, produced by Bulurru Designs Ltd, Australia, c1994. Taylor's dream story painting is entitled 'On Walkabout' and includes footprints.*

and groups are now radically adapting, and even debasing, traditional art forms. Figure 80 illustrates two examples. On the right, the Navajo Indians' traditional sand painting technique has been used to decorate an electric light shade. Beneath it, an Aboriginal design that would previously have been painted on tree bark has been printed on a textile, so that it can be rolled up and transported in a tourist's bag.

As many tourists are reluctant to pay the high cost of time-consuming traditional workmanship, less expensive copies of indigenous arts are sometimes produced in the Far East. These may be sold alongside authentic items, not necessarily to deceive, but to offer the buyer a choice of price.

Whatever one may think of all these recent developments, one thing is clear: there will be no shortage of souvenirs in the next millenium.